# Team Building

## *Current Issues and New Alternatives*

Third Edition

# Team Building

## Current Issues and
## New Alternatives

Third Edition

**William G. Dyer**
*Brigham Young University*

**ADDISON-WESLEY PUBLISHING COMPANY**
*Reading, Massachusetts • Menlo Park, California • New York
Don Mills, Ontario • Wokingham, England • Amsterdam • Bonn
Sydney • Singapore • Tokyo • Madrid • San Juan • Milan • Paris*

**Library of Congress Cataloging-in-Publication Data**

Dyer, William G.
    Team building : current issues and new alternatives / by William
G. Dyer. — 3rd ed.
        p.      cm.    — (Addison-Wesley series on organization
    development)
    Includes bibliographical references.
    ISBN 0-201-62882-1
    1. Work groups.    2. Organizational change.    I. Title.
II. Series.
HD66.D94    1994
658.4'02--dc20
                                                        94-12850
                                                            CIP

This book is in the Addison-Wesley Series on Organization Development.
Editors: Edgar H. Schein, Richard Beckhard

ISBN 0-201-62882-1
    7 8 9 10 BAM 01 00

# Other Titles in the Organization Development Series

## *Creating Labor-Management Partnerships*
Warner P. Woodworth and Christopher B. Meek
1995 (58823)
This book begins with a call for changing the social and political barriers existing in unionized work settings and emphasizes the critical need for union-management cooperation in the present context of international competition. It demonstrates the shift from confrontational union-management relationships toward more effective and positive systems of collaboration. It is written for human resource management and industrial relations managers and staff, union officials, professional arbitrators and mediators, government officials, and professors and students involved in the study of organization development.

## *Competing with Flexible Lateral Organizations, Second Edition*
Jay R. Galbraith
1994 (50836)
This book focuses on creating competitive advantage by building a lateral capability, enabling a firm to respond flexibly in an uncertain world. The book addresses international coordination and cross business coordination as well as the usual cross functional efforts. It is unique in covering both cross functional (lateral or horizontal) coordination, as well as international and corporate issues.

## *Organization Development: A Process of Learning and Changing, Second Edition*
W. Warner Burke
1994 (50835)
This text presents an overview of OD and looks at OD in part as a change of an organization's culture. It looks at the organization and factors that will influence structure and development in the future. The author also introduces new topics such as information management and strategy implementation.

## *The Dynamics of Organizational Levels: A Change Framework for Managers and Consultants*
Nicholas S. Rashford and David Coghlan
1994 (54323)
This book introduces the idea that, for successful change to occur, organizational interventions have to be coordinated across the major levels

of issues that all organizations face. Individual level, team level, inter-unit level, and organizational level issues are identified and analyzed, and the kinds of intervention appropriate to each level are spelled out.

## Total Quality: A User's Guide for Implementation
Dan Ciampa

1992 (54992)

This is a book that directly addresses the challenge of how to make Total Quality work in a practical, no-nonsense way. The companies that will dominate markets in the future will be those that deliver high quality, competitively priced products and service just when the customer wants them and in a way that exceeds the customer's expectations. The vehicle by which these companies move to that stage is Total Quality.

## Parallel Learning Structures: Increasing Innovation in Bureaucracies
Gervase R. Bushe and A.B. Shani

1991 (52427)

Parallel learning structures are technostructural interventions that promote system-wide change in bureaucracies while retaining the advantages of bureaucratic design. This text serves as a resource of models and theories built around five cases of parallel learning structures that can help those who create and maintain them be more effective and successful. For those new to parallel learning structures, the text provides practical advice as to when and how to use them.

## Managing in the New Team Environment: Skills, Tools, and Methods
Larry Hirschhorn

1991 (52503)

This text is designed to help manage the tensions and complexities that arise for managers seeking to guide employees in a team environment. Based on an interactive video course developed at IBM, the text takes managers step by step through the process of building a team and authorizing it to act while they learn to step back and delegate. Specific issues addressed are how to give a team structure, how to facilitate its basic processes, and how to acknowledge differences in relationships among team members and between the manager and individual team members.

*Leading Business Teams: How Teams Can Use Technology and Group Process Tools to Enhance Performance*

Robert Johansen, David Sibbett, Suzyn Benson, Alexia Martin, Robert Mittman, and Paul Saffo

1991 (52829)

What technology or tools should organization development people or team leaders have at their command, now and in the future? This text explores the intersection of technology and business teams, a new and largely uncharted area that goes by several labels, including "groupware," a term that encompasses both electronic and nonelectronic tools for teams. This is the first book of its kind from the field describing what works for business teams and what does not.

*Becoming a Learning Organization: Beyond the Learning Curve*

Joop Sweiringa and André Wierdsma

1991 (62753)

As organizations evolve with time, the ability to learn and change is becoming increasingly more important. The future poses numerous obstacles and challenges for all organizations, and having the proper learning tools will provide a necessary competitive advantage. This text not only analyzes what a learning organization is, it also explores practical approaches and tools that teach a company to "learn to learn." The aim of this book is to identify and define the learning process, but also to begin the implementation of it in order to gain an advantage in a highly competitive environment.

*The Conflict-Positive Organization: Stimulate Diversity and Create Unity*

Dean Tjosvold

1991 (51485)

This book describes how managers and employees can use conflict to find common ground, solve problems, and strengthen morale and relationships. By showing how well-managed conflict invigorates and empowers teams and organizations, the text demonstrates how conflict is vital for a company's continuous improvement and increased competitive advantage.

*Change by Design*

Robert R. Blake, Jane Srygley Mouton, and Anne Adams McCanse

1989 (50748)

This book develops a systematic approach to organization development and provides readers with rich illustrations of coherent planned change.

**vii**

The book involves testing, examining, revising, and strengthening conceptual foundations in order to create sharper corporate focus and increased predictability of successful organization development.

## Organization Development in Health Care
R. Wayne Boss
1989 (18364)

This is the first book to discuss the intricacies of the health care industry. The book explains the impact of OD in creating healthy and viable organizations in the health care sector. Through unique and innovative techniques, hospitals are able to reduce nursing turnover, thereby resolving the nursing shortage problem. The text also addresses how OD can improve such bottom-line variables as cash flow and net profits.

## Self-Designing Organizations: Learning How to Create High Performance
Susan Albers Mohrman and Thomas G. Cummings
1989 (14603)

This book looks beyond traditional approaches to organizational transition, offering a strategy for developing organizations that enables them to learn not only how to adjust to the dynamic environment in which they exist, but also how to achieve a higher level of performance. This strategy assumes that change is a learning process: the goal is continually refined as organizational members learn how to function more effectively and respond to dynamic conditions in their environment.

## Power and Organization Development: Mobilizing Power to Implement Change
Larry E. Greiner and Virginia E. Schein
1988 (12185)

This book forges an important collaborative approach between two opposing and often contradictory approaches to management: OD practitioners who espouse a "more humane" workplace without understanding the political realities of getting things done, and practicing managers who feel comfortable with power but overlook the role of human potential in contributing to positive results.

## Designing Organizations for High Performance
David P. Hanna
1988 (12693)

This book is the first to give insight into the actual processes you can use to translate organizational concepts into bottom-line improvements. Hanna's "how-to" approach shows not only the successful methods of intervention, but also the plans behind them and the corresponding results.

### Process Consultation, Volume 1: Its Role in Organization Development, Second Edition

Edgar H. Schein

1988 (06736)

How can a situation be influenced in the workplace without the direct use of power or formal authority? This book presents the core theoretical foundations and basic prescriptions for effective management.

### Organizational Transitions: Managing Complex Change, Second Edition

Richard Beckhard and Reuben T. Harris

1987 (10887)

This book discusses the choices involved in developing a management system appropriate to the "transition state." It also discusses commitment to change, organizational culture, and increasing and maintaining productivity, creativity, and innovation

### Organization Development: A Normative View

W. Warner Burke

1987 (10697)

This book concisely describes and defines the theories and practices of organization development and also looks at organization development as change in an organization's culture. It is a useful guide to the field of organization development and is invaluable to managers, executives, practitioners, and anyone desiring an excellent overview of this multi-faceted field.

### The Technology Connection: Strategy and Change in the Information Age

Marc S. Gerstein

1987 (12188)

This is a book that guides managers and consultants through crucial decisions about the use of technology for increasing effectiveness and competitive advantage. It provides a useful way to think about the relationship between information technology, business strategy, and the process of change in organizations.

### Stream Analysis: A Powerful Way to Diagnose and Manage Organizational Change

Jerry I. Porras

1987 (05693)

Drawing on a conceptual framework that helps the reader to better understand organizations, this book shows how to diagnose failings in organizational functioning and how to plan a comprehensive set of actions needed to change the organization into a more effective system.

## Process Consultation, Volume II: Lessons for Managers and Consultants

Edgar H. Schein

1987 (06744)

This book shows the viability of the process consultation model for working with human systems. Like Schein's first volume on process consultation, the second volume focuses on the moment-to-moment behavior of the manager or consultant rather than on the design of the OD program.

## Managing Conflict: Interpersonal Dialogue and Third-Party Roles, Second Edition

Richard E. Walton

1987 (08859)

This book shows how to implement a dialogue approach to conflict management. It presents a framework for diagnosing recurring conflicts and suggests several basic options for controlling or resolving them.

## Pay and Organization Development

Edward E. Lawler

1981 (03990)

This book examines the important role that reward systems play in organization development efforts. By combining examples and specific recommendations with conceptual material, it organizes the various topics and puts them into a total systems perspective. Specific pay approaches such as gainsharing, skill-based pay, and flexible benefits are discussed and their impact on productivity and the quality of work life is analyzed.

## Work Redesign

J. Richard Hackman and Greg R. Oldham

1980 (02779)

This book is a comprehensive, clearly written study of work design as a strategy for personal and organizational change. Linking theory and practical technologies, it develops traditional and alternative approaches to work design that can benefit both individuals and organizations.

## Organizational Dynamics: Diagnosis and Intervention

John P. Kotter

1978 (03890)

This book offers managers and OD specialists a powerful method of diagnosing organizational problems and of deciding when, where, and how to use (or not use) the diverse and growing number of organizational improvement tools that are available today. Comprehensive and fully integrated, the book includes many different concepts, research findings, and competing philosophies and provides specific examples of how to use the information to improve organizational functioning.

## Career Dynamics: Matching Individual and Organizational Needs
Edgar H. Schein

1978 (06834)

This book studies the complexities of career development from both an individual and an organizational perspective. Changing needs throughout the adult life cycle, interaction of work and family, and integration of individual and organizational goals through human resource planning and development are all thoroughly explored.

## Matrix
Stanley M. Davis and Paul Lawrence

1977 (01115)

This book defines and describes the matrix organization, a significant departure from the traditional "one man-one boss" management system. The author notes that the tension between the need for independence (fostering innovation) and order (fostering efficiency) drives organizations to consider a matrix system. Among the issues addressed are reasons for using a matrix, methods for establishing one, the impact of the system on individuals, its hazards, and what types of organizations can use a matrix system.

## Feedback and Organization Development: Using Data-Based Methods
David A. Nadler

1977 (05006)

This book addresses the use of data as a tool for organizational change. It attempts to bring together some of what is known from experience and research and to translate that knowledge into useful insights for those who are thinking about using data-based methods in organizations. The broad approach of the text is to treat a whole range of questions and issues considering the various uses of data as an organizational change tool.

## Designing Complex Organizations
Jay Galbraith

1973 (02559)

This book attempts to present an analytical framework of the design of organizations, particularly of types of organizations that apply lateral decision processes or matrix forms. These forms have become pervasive in all types of organizations, yet there is little systematic public knowledge about them. This book helps fill this gap.

## Organization Development: Strategies and Models
Richard Beckhard
1969 (00448)

This book is written for managers, specialists, and students of management who are concerned with the planning of organization development programs to resolve the dilemmas brought about by a rapidly changing environment. Practiced teams of interdependent people must spend real time improving their methods of working, decision making, and communicating, and a planned, managed change is the first step toward effecting and maintaining these improvements.

## Organization Development: Its Nature, Origins, and Prospects
Warren G. Bennis
1969 (00523)

This primer on OD is written with an eye toward the people in organizations who are interested in learning more about this educational strategy as well as for those practitioners and students of OD who may want a basic statement both to learn from and to argue with. The author treats the subject with a minimum of academic jargon and a maximum of concrete examples drawn from his own and others' experience.

## Developing Organizations: Diagnosis and Action
Paul R. Lawrence and Jay W. Lorsch
1969 (04204)

This book is a personal statement of the authors' evolving experience, through research and consulting, in the work of developing organizations. The text presents the authors' overview of organization development, then proceeds to examine issues at each of three critical interfaces: the organization-environment interface, the group-group interface, and the individual-organization interface, including brief examples of work on each. The text concludes by pulling the themes together in a set of conclusions about organizational development issues as they present themselves to practicing managers.

# About the Author

William G. (Bill) Dyer is one of the early practitioners, researchers, and writers in the field of Organization Development. From 1958 to the present, he has combined his academic work in the Brigham Young University School of Management with regular consulting in the organization world. His academic work has produced a dozen books and over 70 articles, instruments, tapes, and manuals. Consulting has taken him to countries around the world and work in business, government, education, religion, and the family. He has held positions as department chair and dean, is president of his own consulting firm, and has served on several boards of directors. His first edition of *Team Building* was the first book written in this important field.

# Foreword

The Addison-Wesley Series on Organization Development origi-
nated in the late 1960s when a number of us recognized that the
rapidly growing field of "OD" was not well understood or well
defined. We also recognized that there was no one OD philosophy, and hence one could not at that time write a textbook on
the theory and practice of OD, but one could make clear what
various practitioners were doing under that label. So the original six books launched what has since become a continuing
enterprise, the essence of which was to allow different authors to
speak for themselves instead of trying to summarize under one
umbrella what was obviously a rapidly growing and highly
diverse field.

By the early 1980s the series included nineteen titles. OD
was growing by leaps and bounds, and it was expanding into all
kinds of organizational areas and technologies of intervention.
By this time, many textbooks existed as well that tried to capture core concepts of the field, but we felt that diversity and
innovation were still the more salient aspects of OD.

Now as we move into the 1990s our series includes over
thirty titles, and we are beginning to see some real convergence
in the underlying assumptions of OD. As we observe how different professionals working in different kinds of organizations and
occupational communities make their case, we see we are still
far from having a single "theory" of organization development.
Yet, a set of common assumptions is surfacing. We are beginning to see patterns in what works and what does not work, and

we are becoming more articulate about these patterns. We are also seeing the field increasingly connected to other organizational sciences and disciplines such as information technology, coordination theory, and organization theory. In the early 1990s we saw several important themes described with Ciampa's *Total Quality* showing the important link to employee involvement in continuous improvement, Johansen et al.'s *Leading Business Teams* exploring the important arena of electronic information tools for teamwork, Tjosvold's *The Conflict-Positive Organization* showing how conflict management can turn conflict into constructive action, Hirschhorn's *Managing in the New Team Environment* building bridges to group psychodynamic theory, and Bushe and Shani's *Parallel Learning Structures* providing an integrative theory for large-scale organization change.

We continue this trend with three revisions and two new books. Burke has taken his highly successful *Organization Development* into new realms with an updating and expansion. Galbraith has updated and enlarged his classic theory of how information management is at the heart of organization design with his new edition entitled *Competing with Flexible Lateral Organizations,* and Dyer has written an important third edition of his classic book on *Team Building.* In addition, Rashford and Coghlan have introduced the important concept of levels of organizational complexity as a basis for intervention theory in their book entitled *The Dynamics of Organizational Levels.* Finally, Woodworth and Meek in *Creating Labor-Management Partnerships* take us into the critical realm of how OD can help in labor relations, an area that's of increasing importance as productivity issues become critical for global competitiveness.

We welcome these revisions and new titles and will continue to explore the various frontiers of organization development with additional titles as we identify themes that are relevant to the ever more difficult problem of helping organizations to remain effective in an increasingly turbulent environment.

*New York, New York*                          Richard H. Beckhard
*Cambridge, Massachusetts*                  Edgar H. Schein

# Preface

In the Preface to the second edition of this book, I emphasized the importance of the commitment of the team leader and team members to spending time building the team. I still feel much the same way about this critical variable in developing successful teams. Since the second edition was published in 1987, however, I have seen so many team-building efforts fail that I am also convinced that it takes more than the commitment of the members of the team for an organizational team to function effectively over time.

I saw one situation in which a company that had been acquired by another company was given the mandate to start a program for putting self-directed work teams into place immediately. No thought was given to whether this was appropriate for the technology, culture, systems, and people of the acquired company. Needless to say, this effort was not seen as successful.

I have watched teams set up to implement Total Quality programs, to create new designs or products, to do strategic planning, but no effort was made to prepare these teams or the team leaders for the work. It is almost assumed that if people are put into a team, they will automatically know how to function.

This indiscriminate use of teams that have not been prepared to function in a team setting and headed by team leaders who have had no real training in team leadership has led me to believe even more strongly that top management must be centrally involved in teamwork. Top management must adopt a true team philosophy and represent that philosophy both in its own performance as well as in written and spoken presentations. Top management must then build rewards and support in all of the organization's review and reward systems in order for people to feel that teamwork and collaboration are truly what the organization is all about. In short, the use of teams, to be successful, must become a part of the culture and structure or systems of the organization.

This book is for managers who want to get a more systematic program of team building moving in their organization or unit. The book is also for professional consultants or human resource specialists who help managers in team-building programs to understand the dynamics of effective team building.

As I have talked with managers and workers over the years, I have been impressed that people do seem to be aware of the unsatisfying nature of work activity that they feel lacks "teamwork" or "team spirit." They may not be able to define clearly what a good team includes, but they have a sense or feeling about a unit that is not working as a team. What do people say about poor teamwork?

> It's no fun working with those people. They just seem to be so involved in their own work that they don't want to do anything for anyone else.
>
> Our meetings are chaos. When we get together and try to get work accomplished, nobody listens—we fight and argue, and nobody supports anyone else.
>
> We never do anything that is teamlike. We don't set goals; we don't plan; we don't work together. Everything is done in one-on-one meetings with the boss. When we have staff meetings, it is just one person at a time talking to the boss while the rest listen.
>
> I don't trust anyone in that bunch I work with. They would all knife you in the back if they thought it would help their cause. At times they can act so friendly, but when the crunch comes, it is each person looking out for Number One.
>
> People talk about teamwork around here, but I don't know what that means. I go to work, I sit at my desk, and I take care of my assignments. From time to time I go to meetings, which are usually a waste of time. I get a yearly

performance review, which hasn't changed much in years, and I draw my pay. I don't see what teamwork means in my job.

There are some people I work with whom I really like and enjoy working with, but there are others who bother me, and we don't get along. I find it easier to avoid them or get things done with as little interaction as possible.

My boss is so busy that he doesn't even talk about how our staff could become a team. He has his favorites whom he talks to, but the rest of us just do our work and hardly ever have any significant involvement with the boss.

Most people have had at least one work experience they felt was "a real good team," and they compare the existing situation with that point of reference in the past. Some people claim that they have *never* been a part of a satisfying work team and do not think they could describe an effective team. It is difficult for people in the latter category to engage in and sustain a team-building program, since they really do not know what they are trying to achieve. People in the first group feel that they know what real teamwork "feels" like, but they are often not sure what kinds of actions are needed to reproduce what they had once experienced.

A critical factor in starting a team-building program is the degree of commitment of the unit manager and members to building a better work team. I have become wary of working with a group on team building if the leader is suspicious, unconvinced, halfhearted, or engaging in the activity because of pressure from above. I want to hear the manager, as he or she talks to the subordinate, say something like

I want this work group to be as good as it can be. Some things go on that keep us from being as effective as we could be. That disturbs me, and it disturbs me that I may be part of the problem. But I am willing to spend my time, energy, and resources to make this group as effective as possible, and I am willing to make needed changes. I need to know how you feel about engaging in a team-building activity. What are your real feelings? I don't think we ought to start unless all of us are truly committed to the activity.

Even with this approach and the commitment of leaders and members, however, the team-building program may fail. Sometimes key people leave; sometimes the problems are too deep or complex. The approach may not be right, or the facilitator may not have enough skill. But without commitment to engage in the process, deeply and honestly, everything could be in order and still nothing would change. So I seek the commitment in my team-building work. I feel that commitment increases if people know what is going to happen and if the process makes sense. But after reviewing the approach and providing all the insight I can, then I want to know about people's commitment. For me, testing commitment is an art, not a science. I cannot measure whether a person is a 6 or an 8 on a commitment scale. I do not have a scale. I have to talk and listen to others talk and trust my experience and judgment. I judge commitment, to some degree, by the willingness of the leader and unit members to take responsibility for team-building work, to spend time, to accept assignments, and to get involved in the agreed-on actions. Team building is a human process involving human feelings, attitudes, and actions. Team building is something that people have to accomplish among themselves. High-paid consultants, complex designs, or fancy resorts are no substitute for human beings making a mutual commitment to try to work together more effectively.

*Provo, Utah*                                                                    W.G.D.

# Contents

**PART I   CURRENT ISSUES IN TEAM BUILDING   1**

**1 Introduction   3**

**2 Organizational Team Building: What Companies Say and What They Do   7**
Team Building in the United States   8
An Agenda for Developing Effective Teams   15
Conclusion   18

**3 Dimensions of Teams   19**
Decision Teams and Task Teams   19
Self-Directed Work Teams   20
Friendship or Trust   21
Degree of Teamwork Needed   22
Team Size   24

**4 Uses of Teams   27**
Special-Issue Teams   27
Self-Directed Work Teams   28
Leadership in Self-Directed Teams   31

**5 Pretended Agreement Versus Constructive Controversy   33**
Unhealthy Agreement   33
Managing Diversity and Making Controversy Constructive   43

**6 Team Development Through Leadership Training   47**
The Shift from Management to Leadership   47
New Leadership Roles   51
Measurement of Team Maturity   58

**7 Building the Collaborative Team Organization 67**
Dimensions of Collaborative Organizations 67
Culture and System Congruence 69
The Individual in the Organization 73
Bringing the Organization into Balance 74

**PART II ALTERNATIVE TEAM-BUILDING DESIGNS 77**

**8 Preparing for Team Building 79**
Is Team Building Needed? 79
Team Building as a Process 81
The Team-Building Cycle 88

**9 Designing a Team-Building Program 93**
Preparation 94
Start-Up 95
Group Problem Solving and Process Analysis 102
Interpersonal, Subunit, and Group Feedback 107
Action Planning 109
Follow-Up 110

**10 Handling Conflict and Confusion in Teams 113**
The Team in Conflict 113
The Team in Confusion 116
The Boss as the Center of Conflict 121
The Problem Member 124

**11 Developing the Temporary Team 127**
Preliminary Conditions for Temporary Teams 127
Design for a New Temporary Team 129

**12 Following Up: What Happens After the Team-Building Session 137**
The Follow-Up Process 137
Follow-Up Team Sessions 140

**13 Reducing Interteam Conflict 143**
Diagnosing the Problem 144
Designing the Solution 144
Choosing an Appropriate Model 148
Conclusions 149

**14 Where Does Team Building Go from Here? 151**

# Part I

# Current Issues in Team Building

# 1

# Introduction

During the ten years between the first edition of this book (1977) and the second edition (1987), rhetoric about the use of teams in organizations became widespread but was not matched by action. Most organizations included in their mission statements, goals, or values their commitment to teamwork, but the systematic building of teams was sporadic. Since 1987, however, the use of teams has almost exploded. A number of trends and issues have emerged along with the increased use of teams.

1. One of the major developments in the field of organization redesign has been the emergence of the self-directed work team. Success by some companies in reorganizing basic work or production units into more self-directed work groups has led to the widespread adoption of this use of teams. Often, however, there has been no study to see if this type of team is suitable. Even more often the teams are set up and put in motion with no training or preparation, and the results have been less than spectacular.

2. In recent years organizations around the world have adopted programs to enhance quality. Total Quality Management (TQM) programs have become commonplace in an increasing number of organizations. Many organizations have tried to improve quality by setting up quality-improvement teams under various labels. These teams have been asked to identify an area in the organization that needs improvement, gather data to

show the current level of low-quality performance, and then propose a new method to improve the quality of the product or process. But too often these teams have been formed without training as to how a team might be effective.

3. Downsizing has become the name of the game in many of the oldest and most respected companies. Exxon, IBM, Sears, Boeing, GM, AT&T, and scores of others have been reducing personnel to be more competitive. This has had a two-fold effect on organizations. On the one hand, many of them are appealing to those people who remain to come together and identify with the company and form "one big team." This attempt to try to develop an organizationwide team feeling has not been very successful. But inside those organizations that downsize, the loss of people has left many who remain with a sense of fear, uncertainty, guilt, and worry, wondering if they might be in the next wave of layoffs. This has led more managers to try to implement a kind of team-building effort to reenergize those people who remain and to give them a sense of cohesion and social support in a work group.

4. A major trend in almost every industry is to venture into the international marketplace. This has meant developing overseas affiliates to handle the new markets or developing a truly multinational organization in which the various parts of a product are produced in various countries, with yet another country as the source of financing, and the major markets in yet different locations. This has led to an increased need to develop teams made up of people of differing backgrounds, cultures, and experiences to do strategic planning for worldwide endeavors. Most organizations have had little experience in building such cross-cultural teams.

5. The importance of employee involvement and participation has increased in the past several years. There is a great deal of data showing how productivity and morale are affected positively when people are personally committed to the decisions and goals of the organi-

zation. This is not a new finding, but the emphasis on developing ways to involve employees in significant ways has increased the trend toward participative management and greater teamwork.

6. Cross-functional teams have been on the rise. When a new product or design is needed, people have been brought out of the traditional departments to help in creative ways to get something new moving ahead. This has led to more and more reliance on matrix organizations and teams made up of people from different functions. This trend, which has existed for many years, seems to be on the increase because of the need for input from several sources, all at the same time, and for maximum creativity in as short a time as possible.

7. Additionally, the need for interdepartmental collaboration remains. Different organizational units that must cooperate with one another often have not learned how to work together as an interteam, collaborative unit.

8. Almost every organization now does "strategic planning." This term has a variety of meanings, depending on the organization. But when a long-term strategy is being developed, the individuals involved in such a planning process must be able to function as an effective team in which diversity of ideas and opinions is desired, conflicts are managed, and plans are made that are both creative and have high commitment from all involved. Too often these top-level strategic-planning groups do not know how to function as effective teams, and the long-term plans they formulate neither are creative nor have high commitment from their members.

These are some of the issues facing those who are using the team concept in organizations today. Some of the problems that teams face have been present from the beginning of the team-building movement. These include dealing with a new, short-term team, often called a task force or committee; a team filled with conflict; a team with a problem leader; and a team that pretends to be in agreement even though many team members privately disagree with actions and decisions that are made.

The chapters that follow will address these and other concerns and try to help managers and facilitators of teams understand the fundamental problems in these areas and give some directions as to possible actions to take.

# 2

# Organizational Team Building

*What Companies Say and What They Do*[1]

When I was conducting a program on team building for 300 managers from the western United States several years ago, I asked the participants, "How many of you feel that effective teamwork is essential to achieve results in your organization?" All present raised their hands. Then I asked, "How many of you currently are engaging in any activity to ensure that the team you manage is functioning effectively?" Fewer than 25 percent raised their hands. Finally I asked, "You belong to another team, one led by your boss. How many of your bosses are doing anything to develop their teams?" This time fewer than 10 percent raised their hands.

Do most organizations give lip service to teamwork, or do they really believe in having effective work teams but simply do nothing to ensure effective team functioning? Given that much of the recent success of Japanese, Korean, and other foreign enterprises can be attributed to their effective use of teams and a set of cultural assumptions that encourage teamwork, I developed a research program to investigate the state of team development and effectiveness in companies in the United States.

---

[1] This chapter was written with the assistance of Dr. W. Gibb Dyer, Jr., of Brigham Young University and Dr. Jeffrey Dyer of the Wharton School of Business, University of Pennsylvania.

## Team Building in the United States

The questions just raised led to a survey of approximately 200 companies across the United States to see if they believed in the importance of building teams, to understand what actions they were taking to develop teams, and if nothing was being done, to understand why not. The survey was sent to personnel and human resource managers in more than a dozen industries, ranging from banking and insurance to aerospace and electronics. Of the 200 surveys sent, usable responses were received from 75—a response rate of about 40 percent.

### Beliefs About Team Building

The results of our survey, although not conclusive about all organizations, do give some insights about the team-building activities in U.S. companies. Initially we were interested in finding out if team development was specifically mentioned in company statements of management philosophy and if their beliefs about how to accomplish the work of their organizations emphasized team building. We asked respondents, "To what extent do you believe that teamwork is needed to accomplish results in your organization?" They could check a response from 1 (not needed at all) to 7 (needed at all times). Ninety-seven percent checked the 5, 6, or 7 level, and 65 percent said that they were at 6 or 7. This confirms the notion that most managers say that teamwork is important.

Respondents were also asked to indicate where teamwork ranked in their companies' priorities, their emphasis of teamwork in company statements of philosophy, and top management's commitment to team building. In terms of company priorities, 47 percent said that teamwork was a high priority, 36 percent said that it was a medium priority, and 17 percent called it a low priority. (It should be remembered that these are the perceptions of mostly personnel or human resource managers.) A number of them wrote in comments, such as, "If you were to ask our top managers, they would say this is a top priority, but in my judgment, it is only medium to low in terms of what is actually being done."

We also asked, "Is teamwork mentioned in any of your company statements of philosophy or goals?" Forty-three percent said that there was a clear, specific statement. Another 33 percent indicated that the importance of teamwork was implied but not mentioned specifically. The other 24 percent said there was no mention about teams in the company statements.

To determine the use of team building as part of performance appraisals, we asked, "Is developing an effective work team part of the requirements in your performance review of managers?" The results follow:

Yes, clearly and specifically:  35%

Yes, implied but not stated:   46%

No, not mentioned:          19%

The personnel/human resource managers were asked, "Do you believe your top corporate management is committed to effective teamwork in your company?" Only 28 percent said that top management was "absolutely committed." Another 40 percent indicated that there was little or no commitment. This points out an interesting paradox, namely, a company's statements may affirm its use of teams even when top management does not support the process.

The answers to these questions suggest, however, that the vast majority of U. S. companies do report that team development is important to the success of their organizations and in some cases attempt to include teamwork as a part of the corporate philosophy or performance appraisal system. This is probably a somewhat optimistic view, given that those responding to the survey are probably likely to be more interested in team building than those who did not respond. What is also apparent, however, is that a significant number of companies tend to neglect team building, failing to include it as part of the corporate philosophy, objectives, or reward system. Moreover, the majority in our survey felt that top management was not fully committed to developing effective teams. Thus many U.S. managers appear to be getting mixed signals about the importance of teamwork.

### *Team-Building Activities*

We were also interested in determining how the respondents defined team building and what kinds of team-building activities were being carried out. Some respondents saw "education" as the way to do team building. Sixty-eight percent said that they had circulated articles or books to their managers that described some aspect of team building. Furthermore, 80 percent indicated that the company had at one time or another used a speaker to describe team-building processes to certain managers in the organization. This ranged from a seminar for top management to a workshop on team building in supervisory or middle-management training programs.

However, when it came to engaging in some team-building activities in their own work groups, such as gathering data about the group's performance and engaging in problem solving, there is much less activity. Only 30 percent indicated that the top-management team spent any considerable time working on its own team development. Another 32 percent said that top management did virtually no team building, and the remaining 38 percent indicated that there had been some action taken at the top level but not to any great extent.

We also attempted to determine how many "work units" (departments, staffs, etc.) in each organization had engaged in some type of team-building activity. Ten percent indicated that as far as they knew, no work unit had ever done any team building. Many responded that to their knowledge, few work groups had ever done any team building. The data seem to be quite clear that most companies in our sample do not engage in active, ongoing team development. In fact, 78 percent indicated that when team building was done, it was a one-time team-building session or event.

Two-thirds of our respondents also indicated that when team building was done, some parts of the organization were more likely to do it than others. Sales and personnel departments were most likely to engage in team development, with engineering and accounting least likely to have a team-building program. It appears as though "people-oriented" functions tend to do team building much more than those with a technical or "numbers" orientation, although we have found in our experience that team development is critical for the success of engineering, manufacturing, and even the accounting functions.

### Why Team Building Is Not Done

We asked our respondents to identify the obstacles to doing team building in their companies. Following is the rank order of the major obstacles listed:

1. Don't know how to do it.
2. Don't understand the rewards.

3. Don't feel it is being rewarded in our company.
4. People feel they don't need it.
5. People feel it takes too much time—not enough time to do it.
6. People feel they do not have the support of their bosses for this activity.

*1. Don't Know How to Do It.* With all of the current emphasis on teamwork, it is interesting to note that the obstacle identified most frequently as most important was a feeling that people in the organization did not know how to go about engaging in a team-building process. Virtually every recent publication on organizations and management has emphasized the importance of effective teams in achieving high levels of performance. However, none of these works describes exactly how these effective teams are developed. There is almost a sense that since everyone agrees that teams are important and almost everyone has participated in some type of team, one must therefore understand how to put an effective team together.

Very few academic programs deal with understanding team processes and dynamics. Students—whether in undergraduate courses or in an M.B.A. program— are assigned to work in teams, and often the team product is graded. However, very few professors know enough or take the time to help these teams deal with the group issues that often occur. Frequently in these class teams, a few students do the work and others coast along and get undeserved credit; in other cases conflicts and problems arise, and because the team does not know how to handle them, the students wind up with strong negative feelings about team effort.

To overcome this lack of skill and knowledge in developing teams, some organizations have a speaker come in and talk about team building or circulate a book or other information. However, most people find it very difficult to start engaging in rather complex activities just by reading or hearing information. They need some experiences, some clear examples of how to do what the information described. The lack of know-how is a major obstacle, but even when people know how to do team building, they still may not take any action if some of the other obstacles are present.

*2. and 3. Don't Understand the Rewards or Team Building Is Not Rewarded.*    Most managers are pragmatic in their approach to taking action. They weigh the possible gains against the down-side risks and usually follow a course of action that will maximize benefits and minimize negative consequences. Many managers we have interviewed have talked about some of the negative effects of team-building programs they have heard about. Some have heard about (but very few have ever directly experienced) team-building efforts resulting in a "bloodbath." They heard that the entire session was devoted to unmercifully giving people harsh, negative feedback. The result was a lot of hard feelings and, if anything, a lessening of team effort. Other horror stories include reported incidents of people quitting or getting fired, a mental breakdown, invasion of people's private lives, or long sessions of people talking about their "feelings" but accomplishing little. With these possible negative effects, coupled with managers' not really understanding how to do team building or clearly seeing the benefits, it is easy to see why many organizations do not engage in formal and ongoing team development.

Another key obstacle is the lack of apparent connections between a team-building effort and the formal rewards in the organization. For many years one major oil company had a program of management development for middle managers. Part of this program included clear instruction about doing effective team building. However, few of these managers implemented their team-development plans on the job. When asked why not, they overwhelming replied that their performance reviews by their bosses did not include anything about team-building efforts. What was emphasized in the management program was not included in either performance reviews or subsequent raises or promotions, and managers could see no organizational payoff for spending the time building the team.

*4. and 5. People Feel They Don't Need It. It Takes Too Much Time.*    Our interviews reveal that because many people have never experienced working in a really effective work team, they have no standard against which to compare their current team. Many describe their current team functioning as "OK," "We're doing all right," or "We are as good as most."

When one couples this attitude with the assumption that the team building is going to eat up a lot of valuable working time, understandably many managers feel that they don't really need team building. Their underlying assumption is that what goes on in team building is not associated with getting work done. It is seen as a kind of "touchy-feely" activity. As one manager said, "What I need is help in getting a lot of work done with reduced manpower. I don't need to waste time while people talk about their feelings."

**6. *Lack of Support from One's Boss.*** Some managers in organizations we studied indicated that even though they would like to engage in team building and felt they knew what to do, they did not get any support for these activities from their bosses. These managers said that their bosses gave the following reasons for not encouraging them to start doing some team-development work:

1. It will take too much time; with our heavy work load, it will have to wait.
2. The boss says his boss doesn't support the notion of team building.
3. Team building is not part of the company goals or the performance review system.
4. We have heard that it is a waste of time.
5. We understand that it requires an outside consultant, and we can't afford that.

### An Effective Team-Building Program

What would a company need to do for team development to have an impact in an organization? Following are the key ingredients of an effective team-building program.

**1. *Top Management Must Provide Clear Support.*** In any organization people at lower levels respond to cues from upper management as to what is truly important in the organization. In their work on leadership W. Bennis and B. Nanus point out that a key issue in leadership is the managing of vision—creating for others a picture of what is possible.[2]

---

[2]W. Bennis and B. Nanus, *Leaders* (New York: Harper and Row, 1985).

A company with a clear, team-related mission statement will assign a top corporate officer or group to continually develop and monitor team action. This sends a clear signal that teams are of fundamental importance and that everyone who is going to succeed must learn to contribute to the team effort. Too many organizations have experienced some team-building emphasis in a middle-management seminar or training program, but there is little evidence that upper management in many organizations takes any of this seriously.

**2.   *Organizational Rewards Should Support Team-work.*** Managers must be able to see that if they develop a successful team, their efforts will be rewarded. This means having some criteria of team effectiveness and having those criteria emphasized in the performance review system.

Managers at all levels should monitor and be monitored as to what they are doing to build effective teams, and organizational resources need to be made available to support such action. Organizations should want the teams to be rewarded with some clear, special rewards, and the teams should not only be allowed but also required to take time out regularly to critique their own team effectiveness and make plans for improvement. Effective teams are singled out for praise in company meetings and in official publications.

It is not necessary to connect pay to team performance, although this is possible, and the process is on the increase, as Dr. Ed Lawler's work on high-involvement management shows.[3] Nonetheless, it is important for managers to see that they are being rewarded for engaging in team-development activities that result in more effective work being done.

**3. *Time for Team Development Should Be Encouraged and Made Available.*** Managers must feel that team building is a high-priority activity and that the organization supports time spent in such a program. If managers feel that upper-level management views team development as a frill that prevents people from getting work done, few people will be inclined to spend time in this area.

---

[3]Edward Lawler, *High Involvement Management* (San Francisco: Jossey-Bass, 1987).

There is some advantage to taking the team away from the work setting for development activities. This is not a requirement, however, and time can be saved if team building is done at the workplace.

*4. People Must Clearly Understand What Team Building Is and What It Is Not.* Most organizational grapevines carry tales about team-building activities being either destructive to some people or a terrible waste of time. The image is that in a team-building session, people sit around and criticize one another, delve into personal matters, or just express their feelings about all kinds of issues, many not related to work.

It should be made clear that the purpose of team building is to help those who must work together to accomplish results, to identify any condition that impedes effective collaboration, and engage in actions that improve the quality of teamwork. The design of a team-building session could be general: (a) What keeps us from being as effective as we could in our work unit? (b) What changes would improve our effectiveness? (c) What are we doing now that is effective that we want to continue? This is a variation on an older format: In order for us to be more effective as a work team, what should we stop doing, start doing, and continue doing?

## An Agenda for Developing Effective Teams

### Identifying Criteria for Effectiveness

If team building is to produce effective teams, it is important to have some criteria for determining what constitutes effectiveness. Our research on organizational work teams has produced the following characteristics of effective teams.

1. Goals and values are clear; they are understood and accepted by everyone. People are oriented to goals and results.

2. People understand their assignments and how their roles contribute to the work of the whole.

3. The basic climate is one of trust and support among members.

4. Communications are open. People are willing and have an opportunity to share all data relevant to the goals of the team and the organization.
5. People are allowed to participate in making decisions. They make free, informed decisions—not decisions they think the "power people" want.
6. Everyone implements decisions with commitment.
7. Leaders are supportive of others and have high personal performance standards.
8. Differences are recognized and handled, not ignored or brushed over lightly.
9. The team structure and procedures are consistent with the task, goals, and people involved.

### Designing a Team-Building Session

These characteristics of effective teams could be used as the basis for developing an agenda of items like the following sample for a team-building session:

1. *Goal setting.* Are people clear about our goals? If not, clarify goals of our unit for the next six months or next year.
2. *Strategic planning.* Where do we want to be in one, three, or five years? What do we need to do to get there?
3. *Expectations.* What do we expect of others on the team? What does each of us need from others to do our job better? What are the manager's expectations of team members?
4. *Decision making.* What are the important decisions being made? Are all relevant people involved appropriately in decisions that affect them?
5. *Organization and assignments.* Do we feel that the unit is organized appropriately? Do we all understand our assignments and how they connect with others? Are people carrying out their assignments effectively?
6. *Morale.* What is the current level of morale in our unit? How could it be improved? Is there a climate of trust and support that everyone feels?

7. *Relations with other units.* How well are we working with other departments?

8. *Communications.* Are we communicating openly all of the information that will help each team member and the team become more effective?

This agenda makes clear that these items are work related. Addressing and handling these issues should help a group of people who must work together to function together more effectively.

The purpose of team-building activities should be clearly explained to the total work unit prior to any action being taken. Everyone should understand that team building is *not* just venting feelings. Team building means frequently taking time to critique performance together and then finding ways to overcome any obstacles and developing more productive patterns of work.

### Undertaking Team Building

First, it should be understood that team building is a process, not an event. If a manager says, "We did team building in 1984," this usually means that after a one-time team-building session was held, the group went back to business as usual.

A team-building program often begins with a one- or two-day session covering an agenda as just described. But the specific design of the program will depend on the issues a team faces. The activities that a conflict-riddled team engages in must differ from those undertaken by a team that is bogged down in complacency or apathy and that needs to be reenergized. The complexity of the team's problem may require the help of an outside consultant or facilitator.

If the major problem is the manager of the unit, an outside person may need to help the manager see when individual improvements are needed and work out a plan of action for the manager. When the team is stifled because of conflicts between two members, it may be more productive to work out these differences outside the group than to take everyone's time in a total-team meeting.

A useful session for any team is to spend some time clarifying each person's role and then having each person describe to others what is needed from them if that person is going to be as effective as possible. When a new team begins to work, it is most helpful for the group to spend time developing a plan for work—what they should do and avoid doing—if they are to be effective. This planning should begin before people plunge into the task.

All teams will find it beneficial to take time out periodically to critique their own effectiveness. Learning how to make corrections in its own functioning is a process that almost any team can learn.

### Conclusion

Clearly these data reveal an imbalance between what people in organizations *say* they are doing about team building and what they *practice*. If organizations are going to use teams effectively, people in power positions must begin to close the gap between what is said and what is done.

# 3

# Dimensions of Teams

It is a truism to say that all teams are not alike. Nonetheless, teams share some key dimensions of structure and function, and these need to be understood if appropriate action for team development is to be taken. Teams have a variety of aspects, or dimensions, which are described in this chapter.

## Decision Teams and Task Teams

Any team has a basic activity and goal. Many teams in organizations have as their basic activity making decisions. People on these decisions teams meet to make decisions about a whole range of matters: defining goals, developing strategy to achieve those goals, giving assignments to a person or unit, allocating resources, cutting or expanding resources for various functions, preparing budgets, setting schedules and deadlines, and so on. It is important for a decision team to understand that the quality and acceptance of the team's decisions can have an immense impact on many other people. For example, if a top-management team is making decisions about downsizing or restructuring and if that group is not open to all information—both hard data, such as the profit picture, and soft data, such as morale—its decisions may be resisted and resented and cause serious problems throughout the total system.

By contrast, members of a work team must, together, perform a set of interlocking tasks in order to accomplish an end result—a certain product, service, or activity. Examples are a production unit that is making a total product (such as a Volvo automobile), a SWAT team, an operating team in a hospital, a NASA space crew, and a utility company service crew.

Obviously work teams must also make decisions, and the quality of those decisions will impact the team's work either positively or negatively. The ability to make effective decisions is thus a key element in all teams. But the work team has the additional function of physically coordinating efforts to achieve a given goal.

Decision teams bog down when team members are working for their own goals and not for the common good or when they do not have access to all of the data. When members go along with power people rather than making decisions based on available data, they make decisions that publicly look like agreement, but in reality members are not willing to implement them. Similarly, these same factors influence the decisions of a work team to appropriately perform the needed functions. In other cases the total team is asked to perform actions the members do not have the time, experience, training, or motivation to accomplish.

## Self-Directed Work Teams

Much of the organization restructuring in recent years is based on the desirability of allowing work teams to have more and more authority to deal with various issues that face them. Such self-directed work teams are also called autonomous and semiautonomous work teams. An autonomous team does not have a formally designated leader. The team can select its own, rotate leadership among members, or operate without a leader—a kind of committee of the whole. The semiautonomous team, by contrast, does have a designated leader with a formal title and position, but the leader's role is defined in such a way that the team makes its own decisions and takes actions independent of the leader. This has led to one of the dilemmas of the semiautonomous team, namely, determining the role of the leader if the team has the right to function without the direct influence and control of that formal leader. Organizations that have successfully adopted this process have begun to redefine the role of the formal leader in some combination of the following:

- The leader functions primarily as a training resource or facilitator to help the team examine how it is working and give the team the needed training, coaching, or facilitation.

- The leader spends most of his or her time dealing with interface issues with other units or with upper management. Or, the leader may increase the interaction and relationships with the customers.

- The leader acts almost like a consultant to the team and can be asked to help deal with team problems, conflicts, problem members, or other concerns.

- The leader may attend all team meetings or attend only when invited. The leader may formally open the meeting but then turn the activities of the meeting over to team members.

It is apparent that some teams are semiautonomous in name only; that is, the formal leader is not willing to relinquish power and continues to function in the traditional leader role of having all activities flow from and through the leader. It should also be apparent that the fully autonomous team can find itself beset with a multitude of problems if the team has never had any training or experience in how to work together as a team. Sometimes these autonomous teams are asked to not only plan, schedule, and coordinate work but also make decisions about hirings, terminations, allocation of pay raises or bonuses, vacation schedules, training needs, or awarding time off to attend meetings or other activities. These issues, which are central to a number of personal concerns of team members, have proved difficult for experienced teams, and an untrained autonomous work team can get buried under a load of activities it is not prepared to handle.

## Friendship or Trust

Members of various teams often ask, Should our goal be to like everyone on the team and to become personal friends with them? A corollary question is, Should we try to select our friends or people we like if we have the opportunity to compose a team? The evidence clearly is that teams whose members have a wide diversity of backgrounds, styles, and experiences have a greater opportunity to be more innovative, creative, and stimulating to other team members. Teams composed of people who are friends or who like one another may spend much of their time trying to keep the good feelings intact and may not be willing to face the disagreements, arguing, confrontation, hammering out of differences, or dealing with other issues that may be critical to productive problem solving or work.

It appears that *trust* is the central factor. One may not like another person's style, mannerisms, or philosophy or values. But the issue for any team member is trust. Can I trust this person to honestly invest in achieving common goals? Can I trust this person to implement decisions or carry out assignments? Can I trust this person to keep confidences? Can I trust this person to give all the data or information that person has? Can I trust this person to stay in relationships and work out disagreements? Can I trust this person to come to the assistance of another person who may need support?

The evidence is that people who trust one another can work together productively and effectively on a team. In fact, the building of trust should be a key goal for any team. Trust is the glue that keeps team members working together; when trust is lost, it is very difficult to regain. One of the only ways to regain trust is to confront the distrustful person or issue directly. When that loss of trust is recognized, the person(s) involved must own up to the condition and be willing to work to correct the matter and have the issue open for further discussion.

### Degree of Teamwork Needed

Although all teams represent a collection of people who must collaborate, *to some degree,* to achieve common goals, there is a difference in the amount of collaboration required. Figure 3.1 represents a continuum of teamwork or collaboration needed for a team to function.

Some teams are not required by the nature of the task to work closely together all the time. For example, a golf team may do some general strategy planning and share information, but in the final analysis play is by the individual performer. Similarly, an academic department requires relatively little teamwork. Each professor can do most of the required work—teach, research, write—alone. When important decisions need to be made or departmental goals set that require coordinated efforts of

**Figure 3.1**
*Continuum of Teamwork*

| Low teamwork | | Average teamwork | | | High teamwork | |
|---|---|---|---|---|---|---|
| 1 | 2 | 3 | 4 | 5 | 6 | 7 |
| Golf Team | | Baseball Team | | | Basketball Team | |
| University Dept. | | Accounting Dept. | | | NASA Space Team | |
| | | | | | SWAT Team | |

all department members, then they must function as a decision team. However, these times occur at fairly well-spaced intervals.

Other teams must meet together more regularly and consistently coordinate their work. An accounting or financial department in a company is an example. Everyone who works in such a department must show a common accounting framework, and the work of one part of the accounting financial process depends on the work of other parts. The accuracy of the tax people depends in part on how well internal auditors have done their work. Although each accountant may be doing individual work, one may sometimes not be able to proceed without input from others.

Most company executive committees require an average amount of teamwork. For much of their work, the heads of marketing, finance, personnel, and manufacturing can work autonomously in their own areas. But at key times they must come together and build a common strategy, set common goals, and work out certain conditions, such as getting marketing and manufacturing to agree on the type and amount of product that should be produced for the marketplace.

A baseball team is another example of an average teamwork situation. All nine players must be on the field at once, but for most of the game, the effort is individual in nature; each player bats, runs, and fields alone. Only the catcher and pitcher interact constantly, and a few others must rely on each other in a double play or infield out.

In some groups the nature of the task requires a high degree of teamwork. Members of a basketball team are on the court all together, all of the time. All members must do everything—run, shoot, play defense. Every member interacts with every other member. Thus one would predict that a basketball team would suffer more from the lack of teamwork than would a golf or track team.

When an Air Force bomber flies a mission, every member of the crew has a specific set of assignments that are critical if the venture is to be successful. Every person depends on everyone else. Such is also the case for a police SWAT team or the team of people in a hospital operating room. All of the tasks are highly connected and members cannot do their respective work without others doing theirs.

## Team Size

What is the optimal size of an effective team? There is no clear answer to that question. A team may be two people playing doubles in tennis, or a team may be players functioning alone, as on a golf team. The golfers meet together, give feedback to one another, and provide mutual support and encouragement. They also are working to become the champions of their league and so have common goals. In that sense they are as much a team as a group of players on a basketball team.

Currently there are strong attempts in very large organizations, such as General Motors, to get all employees to have a sense of identity with the whole organization as a "team." If you could get several thousand employees all identifying with the same set of goals, sharing the same vision, and working to support every other person with whom they work, would you have a real team?

Many attempts have been made to describe the central dimensions of a team. Some of these central dimensions are:

- *Face-to-face interaction and mutual influence.* This dimension would preclude a larger group with common goals but no face-to-face interaction.

- *Interdependence and structured relationships.* This dimension is more inclusive, and many people in organizations are interdependent. If and when they interact, the relationships are structured or defined, but they do not interact face to face.

- *Perceived membership.* Some have felt that people are part of a team if they identify with the team and feel connected to it. Are people who identify with the Notre Dame football team and who contribute financially to the football program part of a larger, loosely knit team?

- *Common goals and tasks.* Ford Motor Company might meet this criterion. The employees may share common goals, and ideally their tasks all unite to achieve those goals.

There probably is a difference between a team whose members interact and one whose members share identification and common vision or goals. But even at the interacting level, it is not clear how many people can interact effectively at one time. I have done team building with a husband and wife, with a management group of three, and with a department of twenty. The nature of the interaction of the team is different, depending on the size, and the methods of team building may change, but size does not seem to be the critical factor in determining a team or how to build it.

# 4

# Uses of Teams

In the past several years the use of teams has proliferated in a wide variety of organizations. Self-directed work teams (also called autonomous or semiautonomous work teams) have been organized as a basic unit in many organizational reengineering efforts. Often teams have been formed to work on improving quality. Known as quality-improvement teams (QIT), continuous-improvement teams (CIT), or total quality teams (TQT), for example, these quality-oriented teams have often been formed as part of total quality management (TQM) programs.

Additionally, cross-functional design teams, which draw members from existing functional departments, have frequently been used for the purpose of creating a new design or a new procedure or to solve a particular technical or organizational problem. Recently strategic planning has been central to many organizations, especially those considering downsizing, changing directions, or moving into new markets. This has led to the formation of many strategic planning teams. This chapter focuses on these new, varied uses of teams and what happens when they succeed or fail.

## Special-Issue Teams

The use of teams to deal with matters of quality, cross-functional problems, and strategic planning is consistent with the notion that a team strategy is appropriate when a variety of human resources must be brought together to solve a particular problem. The major roadblock to the effective functioning of such decision teams is that usually there is no time taken to prepare the members to function as a team. The team leader needs to understand something of the demands of this particular role and be prepared to spend time building a team mentality and some team skill, rather than plunging immediately into work. All of these special-issue teams should follow the format described in Chapter 11 for temporary teams.

An important issue in using teams for quality, design, or strategic purposes is whether a new team should be formed or whether the problems should instead be solved in existing units. For example, one oil company implemented a program to improve quality by establishing new teams to work on quality problems. But two problems occurred. First, the new teams were not given any training on how they were to function, and they began to run into serious process problems (conflicts, low attendance, apathy, jealousies, etc.) that neither the team leader nor members could handle. Second, it soon became apparent that managers were being evaluated on the number of quality teams they had established. One's rating was enhanced or diminished on the basis of how many quality teams one could report. The result was that managers were setting up all kinds of teams in order to look good, but the teams were not accomplishing anything of significance. The company had not examined the primary issue first, namely, whether quality problems should be solved by existing departments or work units or by new teams formed for that purpose. When the strategy of forming new teams was adopted, existing departments assumed that quality was the domain of the new teams, not theirs.

Such results suggest that rather than setting up a new, parallel stream of teams, existing units should be the first line of action, particularly if they are seriously involved in the area of concern. New teams should be established only when the problem or issue cuts across different departments and resources from the several departments are needed. To optimize the new team's chance of succeeding, adequate training or orientation should be given to both the team and the team leader.

## Self-Directed Work Teams

Although quality remains a popular issue in organizations around the world, organization redesign has emerged as an issue for attention. The basic proposition is that organizations should be designed around processes rather than functions. In handling processes the basic production unit is the team, not the individual. Furthermore, these teams are "self-directed"; that is, they do not require a traditional supervisor but instead are responsible for the total work of the team. Whether semiautonomous, indicating the inclusion of a formally designed leader, or autonomous, meaning that the group handles all of its own leadership matters, these teams are responsible for taking inputs (raw materials, raw data) and transforming or converting them into a more finished condition. The team sets its own work goals, establishes schedules and time frames for work, trains its people, and may even be asked to handle matters of hiring, evaluating team members, recommending pay increases or bonuses, and terminating noneffective team members. The team may also deal with its own needs for materials and supplies, handle its own quality control, and generally be responsible for functions that were formerly handled by other departments (purchasing, maintenance, quality control, personnel, etc.) The successes of these newly redesigned organizations and the effectiveness of these self-directed work teams have been widely reported.[1]

What makes these self-directed work teams different from and more effective than other teams? Paul Gustafson, a consultant who has worked with a number of companies in redesigning work, identifies several key factors in a successful self-directed work team.[2]

1. *The team must be responsible for a total conversion or transformation process.* This means the team must be able to take some kind of input and transform it into a more complete entity. The team must be able to see the transformation take place as a result of its efforts. The classic example of this conversion process is the team that built the total Volvo automobile. The conversion

---

[1] See Thomas A. Stewart, "The Search for the Organization of Tomorrow," *Fortune*, May 18, 1992:93–98; Thomas A. Stewart, "Reengineering the Company," *Fortune*, Aug 23, 1993 40–45; and Michael Hammer, "Reengineering Work: Don't Automate, Obliterate," *Harvard Business Review*, July–Aug 1990:104–112.)

[2] Gustafson's work at American Transtech is described in S. Keil, "Designing America's New Corporate Culture," *The Tarrytown Letter*, Tarrytown, N.Y., April 1985.

does not have to be on that large a scale, but when the team examines its work, it must see that it has created or added something new.

2. The team must have available an ongoing source of relevant information. For example, through the use of computers made available to the team, team members see almost continuously their productivity, quality, profitability, supply sources, inventories, and so on. Only by having such information available on demand can the team make necessary adjustments in its operations or change short-term goals or shift team resources and skills.

3. *The team must have available needed technical, business, and interpersonal skills.* Technical skills are those needed to handle the equipment, technology, or operations involved in the process. Team members are often encouraged and rewarded to learn a wide variety of technical skills so that team members are interchangeable. Business skills are those related to handling business information—reports on quality, profitability of the team's efforts against larger production and profit goals, and computer printouts. Interpersonal skills are those needed to function effectively with the other team members to make good decisions, handle differences, resolve conflicts if they arise, build trust, share data openly, give and receive feedback, assume leadership activities as needed, supply needed muscle and emotional support to other team members, and subordinate personal objectives to team goals as appropriate.

   The necessary mix of these skills must either be anticipated as the team is formed and members are recruited because of their skill mix, or there must be a method for those with some skills to teach others these skills. Unfortunately, sometimes self-directed work teams are formed, but no program is in place to teach team members the needed skills or to put in place the needed collaborative processes.

4. *There is continual interaction between the team and the customer(s).* Part of the new design includes the process flow that the self-directed work team creates a convert-

ed product for a customer. The work team is responsible to its customers, who can be either inside or outside the company. Teams do not work on an isolated product but rather on an outcome that is important to a "customer." Thus every team is responsible for making a transformed product and is also responsible to a customer. These dual responsibilities are designed to increase the sense of commitment of the team to achieve its goals.

The team, either directly by all team members or through the team leader or representative, is in continual touch with the customer. Thus the team gets feedback about the customer's level of satisfaction and input about any needed changes.

5. *The work of the team is directly connected to the reward system of the organization.* Research evidence clearly shows that people must see that their efforts are appreciated and rewarded in both the formal and informal parts of the organization. Different kinds of reward systems are being used. Some companies reward both individual and team efforts. Individuals can be rewarded by "pay for performance or skill." As the person demonstrates increased competence, the pay rate is increased accordingly. The team also gets rewarded, often in the form of profit sharing or a bonus distributed among team members. Attempts are made to connect all forms of reinforcement to the worker: enriched job, team support, personal development, immediate feedback on performance, praise from customers, and financial gain.

Gustafson contends that all five conditions must be present in order for self-directed work teams to be effective. If any is missing, the ability of the team to function on its own is seriously diminished.

## Leadership in Self-Directed Teams

In the traditional leadership role the supervisor is in control and conducts meetings, sets goals, makes assignments, conducts performance reviews, and allocates rewards. These functions are relegated to the self-directed work team itself, which may or may not have a designated leader. But if the leader of a semiautonomous work team is no longer "in control," what does that person do? This issue has been discussed in two recent books.[3]

These writers and others who have looked at the leadership issue in self-directed work teams all agree that the person in this new role must begin to behave in a whole new set of ways. First, this leader must abandon traditional notions of the role of the leader/supervisor and instead develop a whole new philosophy of leadership. Second, the leader must learn to function more as an educator, coach, and facilitator, as described in Chapter 6. Third, the leader must develop a different relationship with team members, and must be regarded as a useful resource rather than as someone in charge. This is sometimes difficult, for in a sense that leader is functioning best when the team does not need the leader's help in order to function effectively. If the team leader has strong needs for centrality, visibility, and personal recognition, this new role may be difficult to assume.

The new dimension of this leader's job must be in activities outside the regular dynamics of the team. Since the effective work team is handling most of its internal affairs, this should leave the team leader to deal with external relationships. The leader should now have time to increase interaction with those in power positions above and to deal with interface issues with other teams, departments, and functions. If it is appropriate, the leader could be a primary contact with customers. In this external role the leader represents the team, feeds data back to the team from these outside contacts, and helps the team develop a process for dealing with this wider environment.

Again, one of the weak points in establishing self-directed work teams has been the inadequate selection and training of team leaders, if in fact one is needed. Some type of team leadership training, such as described in Chapter 6, should be part of the preparation of the self-directed work team.

---

[3]Kimball Fisher, *Leading Self-Directed Work Teams* (New York: McGraw-Hill, 1993) and John Zenger *et al., Leading Teams* (Homewood, Ill.: Business One Irwin, 1994).

# 5

# Pretended Agreement Versus Constructive Controversy

This chapter was originally written with Jerry Harvey and contains his discussion of the Abilene Paradox—the now famous analysis of groups of people who make public decisions that seem to reflect total agreement, although few, if any, of the team members feel that the decisions are appropriate. The original case situation and discussion are presented again, for groups caught in the web of unhealthy agreement are still around, and breaking out of this dilemma is an important issue for them. However, the reverse side of the matter has become a wider concern, namely, how to deal with diversity and encourage and then manage differences of all kinds and even make controversy constructive. This chapter deals with the team that pretends to be in agreement but truly is not, as well as with teams that are widely diverse and need to learn to become effective in the midst of controversy.

## Unhealthy Agreement

At times teams bog down, not out of conflict that is open but because people pretend to agree when in fact they do not, as illustrated by the incident described in the next section.

### The Abilene Paradox[1][2]

July Sunday afternoons in Coleman, Texas (population 5607) are not exactly winter holidays. This one was particularly hot—104 degrees as measured by the Walgreen's Rexall Ex-Lax Temperature Gauge located under the tin awning that covered a rather substantial "screened-in" back porch. In addition, the wind was blowing fine-grained West Texas topsoil through what were apparently cavernous but invisible openings in the walls.

"How could dust blow through closed windows and solid walls?" one might ask. Such a question betrays more of the provincialism of the reader than the writer. Anyone who has ever lived in West Texas wouldn't bother to ask. Just let it be said that wind can do a lot of things with topsoil when more than thirty days have passed without rain.

But the afternoon was still tolerable—even potentially enjoyable. A water-cooled fan provided adequate relief from the heat as long as one didn't stray too far from it, and we didn't. In addition, there was cold lemonade for sipping. One might have preferred stronger stuff, but Coleman was "dry" in more ways than one; and so were my in-laws, at least until someone got sick. Then a teaspoon or two for medicinal purposes might be legitimately considered. But this particular Sunday no one was ill; and anyway, lemonade seemed to offer the necessary cooling properties we sought.

And finally, there was entertainment. Dominoes. Perfect for the conditions. The game required little more physical exertion than an occasional mumbled comment, "shuffle 'em" and an unhurried movement of the arm to place the spots in the appropriate perspective on the table. It also required somebody to mark the score; but that

---

[1]Much of the material in the section entitled "The Abilene Paradox" was contained in the article by J. Harvey, "Managing Agreement in Organizations: The Abilene Paradox." Reprinted by permission of the publisher from *Organizational Dynamics*, Summer 1974. © 1974 by AMACOM, a division of the American Management Association. It is also found in Harvey's book, *The Abilene Paradox and Other Meditations on Management* (Lexington, Mass: Lexington Books, 1988).  .

[2]With Jerry Harvey.

responsibility was shifted at the conclusion of each hand so the task, though onerous, was in no way physically debilitating. In short, dominoes was diversion, but pleasant diversion.

So, all in all it was an agreeable—even exciting—Sunday afternoon in Coleman; if, to quote a contemporary radio commercial, "You are easily excited." That is, it was until my father-in-law suddenly looked up from the table and said with apparent enthusiasm, "Let's get in the car and go to Abilene and have dinner at the cafeteria."

To put it mildly, his suggestion caught me unprepared. You might even say it woke me up. I began to turn it over in my mind. "Go to Abilene? Fifty-three miles? In this dust storm? We'll have to drive with the lights on even though it's the middle of the afternoon. And the heat. It's bad enough here in front of the fan, but in an unairconditioned 1958 Buick it will be brutal. And eat at the cafeteria? Some cafeterias may be okay, but the one in Abilene conjures up dark memories of the enlisted men's field mess."

But before I could clarify and organize my thoughts even to articulate them, Beth, my wife, chimed in with, "Sounds like a great idea. I would like to go. How about you, Jerry?" Well, since my own preferences were obviously out of step with the rest, I decided not to impede the party's progress and replied with, "Sounds good to me," and added, " I just hope your mother wants to go."

"Of course I want to go," my mother-in-law replied. "I haven't been to Abilene in a long time. What makes you think I wouldn't want to go?"

So into the car and to Abilene we went. My predictions were fulfilled. The heat was brutal. We were coated with a fine layer of West Texas dust, which was cemented with perspiration by the time we arrived; and the food at the cafeteria provided first-rate testimonial material for Alka-Seltzer commercials.

Some four hours and 106 miles later, we returned to Coleman, Texas, but tired and exhausted. We sat in front of the fan for a long time in silence. Then, both to be sociable and also to break a rather oppressive silence, I said, "It was a great trip, wasn't it?"

No one spoke.

Finally, my mother-in-law said, with some slight note of irritation, "Well, to tell the truth, I really didn't enjoy it much and would have rather stayed here. I just went along because the three of you were so enthusiastic about going. I wouldn't have gone if you hadn't all pressured me into it."

I couldn't believe it. "What do you mean 'you all?'" I said, "Don't put me in the 'you all' group. I was delighted to be doing what we were doing. I didn't want to go. I only went to satisfy the rest of you characters. You are the culprits."

Beth looked shocked. "Don't call me a culprit. You and Daddy and Mama were the ones who wanted to go. I just went along to be sociable and to keep you happy. I would have had to be crazy to want to go out in heat like that. You don't think I'm crazy, do you?"

Before I had the opportunity to fall into that obvious trap, her father entered the conversation again with some abruptness. He spoke only one word, but he did it in the quite simple, straightforward vernacular that only a lifelong Texan and particularly a Colemanite can approximate. That word was "H-E-L-L-L."

Since he seldom resorted to profanity, he immediately caught our attention. Then he proceeded to expand on what was already an absolutely clear thought with, "Listen, I never wanted to go to Abilene. I was sort of making conversation. I just thought you might have been bored, and I felt I ought to say something. I didn't want you and Jerry to have a bad time when you visit. You visit so seldom, I wanted to be sure you enjoyed it. And I knew Mama would be upset if you all didn't have a good time. Personally, I would have preferred to play another game of dominoes and eaten the leftovers in the icebox."

After the initial outburst of recrimination, we all sat back in silence. Here we were, four reasonable, sensible people who, on our own volitions, had just taken a 106-mile trip across a Godforsaken desert in furnacelike temperatures through a cloudlike dust storm to eat unpalatable food at a hole-in-the-wall cafeteria in Abilene, Texas, when none of us really wanted to go. In fact, to be more accurate, we'd done just the opposite of what we wanted to do. The whole situation seemed paradoxical. It simply didn't make sense.

At least it didn't make sense at that time. But since that fateful summer day in Coleman, I have observed, consulted with, and been a part of more than one organization that has been caught in the same situation. As a result, it has either taken a temporary side-trip, and occasionally, a terminal journey to Abilene when Dallas or Muleshoe or Houston or Tokyo was where it really wanted to go. And for most of those organizations, the destructive consequences of such trips, measured both in terms of human misery and economic loss, have been much greater than for the Abilene group.

This story is concerned with a paradox, "The Abilene Paradox." Stated simply, it is as follows: Organizations frequently take actions in contradiction of what they really want to do and therefore defeat the very purposes they are trying to achieve. It also deals with a major corollary of the paradox, which is that *the inability to manage agreement is a major source of dysfunction* in organizations from the team level up to the total organization.

When a team gets lost in such a cloud of unrecognized agreement, it frequently manifests behavior that leads one to believe, mistakenly, that the unit is caught in a dilemma of conflict. For that reason, it takes a different type of team-development, problem-solving process—one involving agreement management—to develop new, more functional organizational behaviors.

### Symptoms of the Problem

Since the surface symptoms (that is, conflict) of both agreement and disagreement are essentially similar, the first requirement is to be aware of the symptoms of an agreement-management dilemma. Then, on the basis of correctly identifying the symptoms, one can take functional corrective action.

Harvey[3] has identified two sets of symptoms. The first set can most easily be identified by someone outside the system under scrutiny. In effect, being free of the blinding forces of action anxiety, negative fantasies, existential risk, and the psy-

---

[3]J. Harvey. "Managing Agreement in Organizations: The Abilene Paradox." *Organizational Dynamics* (Summer 1974):63–80.

chological reversal of risk and certainty, all of which contribute
to the paradox's pernicious influence, the outsider can frequently
observe symptoms hidden by the dust that is all too familiar to
residents of Abilene.

The second set, more subjective in character, can be more
easily recognized by persons living within the system.

### Symptoms More Easily Observable to Outsiders.

Outsiders, whether detached laypeople or professional consultants,
can be relatively sure that the team is on a trip to Abilene if
they observe the following symptoms:

1. Team members feel pain, frustration, feelings of impotence or sterility when trying to cope with the problem.
   In gross terms, there is a lot of apparent conflict.

2. Members agree privately, as individuals, as to the
   nature of the problem facing the organization.

3. Members also agree, privately, as individuals, as to the
   steps required to cope with the problem.

4. There is a great deal of blaming others for the conditions they are in.

5. People break into subgroups of trusted friends to share
   rumors, complaints, fantasies, or strategies relating to
   the problem or its solution.

6. In collective situations (group meetings, public memoranda) members fail to communicate their desires and
   beliefs to others accurately. In fact, they frequently
   communicate just the opposite of what they mean.

7. On the basis of such invalid and inaccurate information, members make collective decisions that lead them
   to take actions contrary to what they personally and
   collectively want to do.

8. As a result of such counterproductive actions, members
   experience even greater anger, frustration, irritation,
   and dissatisfaction with the organization.

9. Members behave differently outside the organization.
   In other situations (families, churches, other work
   units) they are happier, get along better with others,
   and perform more effectively.

*Symptoms More Easily Observable to Insiders.* Similarly, some symptoms, stemming primarily from one's subjective experiences within the team, are more easily identified by persons who are caught up in the problem of mismanaged agreement. For example, if you experience the following feelings within your work unit, you may be pretty sure that you are lost in a dust storm of agreement and are on a trip to Abilene:

1. You feel pained, frustrated, impotent, sterile, and basically unable to cope when trying to solve a particular organizational problem.

2. You frequently meet with trusted associates over coffee, clandestine lunches, or in the privacy of your home or office to discuss the problem, to commiserate, and to plan fantasized solutions that you would attempt "if the conditions were only right." (Fortunately, or unfortunately, depending on your point of view, they seldom are.)

3. You blame others, the boss, other divisions, or those "unperceptive people in unit X" for the dilemma. The boss, in particular, frequently gets an unequal share of the blame and is described with such statements as, "He's out of touch," "She's lost control of the unit," or "He sure as heck isn't as good as Mrs. Watson in dealing with problems like this."

4. In collective meetings at which the problem is discussed, you are frequently cautious, less than candid, and vague when discussing your ideas regarding the problem and its solution. Stated differently, you frequently try to determine what others' positions on the issues are without clearly revealing your own.

5. You repeatedly find that the problem-solving actions you take, both individually and collectively, not only fail to solve the problem but also tend to make it worse.

6. You frequently hold fantasized conversations with yourself on what you might have done—or should have done—"When he said..., I wish I had said....."

7. Finally, you frequently look for ways to escape by taking sick leave or vacation time, traveling, or scheduling other, "more important" meetings on days when the problem is going to be discussed.

Only when someone in the work unit becomes aware of either or both sets of symptoms does it become possible to design a problem-solving process designed to break out of what is ultimately a self-defeating organizational process.

### *Team Development Around the Crises of Agreement*

Since an essential cause of the hidden-agreement syndrome is that team members are afraid to "own up"[4] to their basic concerns, coping with hidden agreement in work groups is especially difficult. That difficulty, in turn, stems from three essential dilemmas. (1) It involves risk and takes skill for an individual to "own up" to his or her true feelings and beliefs about an issue when other members of the team have publicly taken different or contrary positions. (2) It involves risk and takes skill for others to "own up" to their similar private feelings and beliefs, because of their negative fantasies of the terrible consequences that might occur if they reveal them in an unequivocal manner. (3) It is very difficult to learn the individual and collective skills required, even if one is willing to accept the risks.[5]

In summary, the possibility that a work unit could exhibit public equanimity, private turmoil, and perform ineffectively is one compelling reason for work groups to hold periodic team review and development sessions when symptoms of the Abilene Paradox are present. Another reason is that the organization might be able to do something constructive about the problem, even though the skills required for success in such a session may not be easy or comfortable to learn.

### *Format Possibilities for Agreement-Management Team-Development Sessions*

A number of possible formats exist for taking action to solve problems. Generally they involve gathering data, sharing theory, and setting norms. Data gathering may be conducted by either insiders or outside consultants.

---

[4]The term "own up" has a very precise meaning. Essentially, *owning up* is (1) a first-person statement beginning with the word *I* ("I think," "I believe," "I want") in which the individual (2) clearly communicates his or her own ideas and feelings about an issue (3) in a descriptive way (4) without attributing an idea, a feeling, a belief, or a motivation to another.

[5]See C. Argyris, *Intervention Theory and Method: A Behavioral Science Approach* (Reading, Mass.: Addison-Wesley, 1970), and C. Argyris and D. Schon, *Theory in Practice* (San Francisco: Jossey-Bass, 1974).

***Data Collection by an Outside Consultant.*** To bring
hidden agreements to light, it may be useful to have an outside
consultant interview people in the organization unit. (An "outside" consultant is someone who is not a part of the blinding, col-
lusive anxiety system that facilitates the hidden-agreement
syndrome and who knows the theory and practice of agreement
management; in other words, he or she may be a competent professional, friend, or colleague.) Based on the theory of agreement
management, such a consultant might ask the following questions: (1) What problem does this organizational unit have that
you have a hard time accepting, facing, or discussing? (The question assumes that the respondent knows the nature of the problem and can state it.) (2) What decisions or actions that you have
not really agreed with have recently been taken regarding the
problem? (The question helps determine whether there are consistent discrepancies between private beliefs and public actions,
a key symptom of an agreement-management dilemma.) (3)
What actions or decisions do you feel would produce the best
results for the organization over the long term? (The question
assumes that the respondent knows an effective solution to the
problem.) (4) What will happen if you don't discuss your concerns, feelings, beliefs, and suggestions with all members of the
unit who are involved with the problem? What will happen if you
do? (The questions assume that fantasized consequences will
either help or hinder the individual's making a decision to discuss the issue with others in such a way that the problem might
be solved.)

Having gathered the data through interviews, the outside
consultant would then present a summary of their responses
simultaneously to them in a group problem-solving session,
designed and "contracted" for, essentially, in the manner
described by Beckhard,[6] Burke,[7] and Schein.[8]

[6]R. Beckhard, "The Confrontation Meeting," *Harvard Business Review*
(March–April 1967):149–155.

[7]W. Warner Burke, *Organization Development: A Process of Learning and
Changing, Second Edition* (Reading, Mass.: Addison-Wesley, 1994). See especially Chapter 4.

[8]E. H. Schein, *Process Consultation, Vol. 1, Second Edition* (Reading,
Mass.: Addison-Wesley, 1988).

*Data Collection by Members of the Organization.*   It
is also possible that within the organization, people who are a
part of the problem could share data and, by exhibiting such
behavior, could encourage others to do the same. In this case an
outside interviewer would not be needed. Again, such data are
most effectively shared in a group meeting involving all people
key to the problem. In such a meeting the person who called the
meeting explains his or her desire to "own up" and expresses a
desire to know others' beliefs and feelings about the issue. A typ-
ical statement at the beginning of such a meeting might be as follows: "I have some data I want to share with you. I'm anxious
about doing it because I may find I'm the only one who sees the
problem this way, and I don't like to feel alone. But here it is. I
really don't think we are going to succeed on project X. It's important for me to know how others feel about it, though. I would
appreciate your letting me know what you think." Despite the
competence and good intentions of the person making such a
statement, the fear element might still be so strong that other
members of the organization would be unwilling to reveal their
true beliefs and feelings. It is also possible, however, that at least
one person would "own up" to his or her concerns and the log jam
would be broken. Alternatively, in the absence of such "owning"
statements the probability of the problems being solved is
reduced.

*Sharing the Theory and Taking Action.*   In addition
to collecting and sharing data, another important element of
such problem-solving sessions is for all members of the organization to know the theory of agreement management. To accomplish the goal of communicating theory, the story of the "Abilene
Paradox," which opens this chapter, could be distributed to all
members of the group prior to the problem-solving meeting. Each
person could be asked to read the story and be ready to discuss
whether he or she had ever experienced, observed, or even fore-
seen any situation in which the organization was or might be in
danger of taking a trip to Abilene, that is, doing something that
no one really wanted to do or not doing something organization
members really wanted to do. At the problem-solving meeting
each person could be asked to discuss the Abilene Paradox and
his or her observations of its relevance to the work group. Since
the reactions of authority figures set the parameters of other

responses in any type of confrontation meeting, it is helpful if the head of the organization can begin the process and can "own up" to personal concerns about any trips to Abilene that he or she has observed, participated in, led, or may foresee leading. Once the work group has discussed the theory of hidden agreements and has shared data about any potential agreements that they may be incorrectly treating as conflicts, it is important to come to valid public agreement about the nature of the "true" conditions, make action plans based on the reality of such truths, and then take steps to reduce the probability of future trips to Abilene.

## Managing Diversity and Making Controversy Constructive

The flip side of the Abilene Paradox is the highly diverse team whose problem is not false agreements but differences that are so apparent and so open, one wonders if it is possible to come to any agreements to which all members will be committed. These diverse teams are a result of several forces moving on today's organizations. There is the demand on the part of various groups (women, African-Americans, Hispanics, Native Americans, the aging, and others) to be treated fairly and to be included in the decision-making and power structures. More and more, these groups are being represented in decision-making teams. Business organizations are crowding one another to become international and to capture foreign markets. This means more multicultural planning and policy-making groups. Factions formerly in adversarial positions are now trying to work together collaboratively: management, labor, government, environmental groups, consumer groups, the media, among many others. Along with these diverse groupings, people are now owning publicly the wide range of factors that distinguish them from others—age, race, ethnic origin, social status, education, religion, political affiliation, gender, family status, regional identification, personal style, personal experiences, and so on. All of this means that when any people come together as a "team," there is immediately present a range of diversity that leaders are recognizing as a great strength and not a drawback to effective work. Most of the research on groups that use diversity productively shows that these groups are innovative and creative; members are more sensitive and appreciative of others who are different and who have different skills and personal resources.[9]

When diversity is not controlled or used effectively, differences can split people apart, cause endless arguments and bickering, and result in bitter feelings, resentments, and less productive work. The issue is how to make diversity work in a positive way to capitalize on the richness of difference that is in every team.

When team members have obvious differences, one of their goals should be to achieve a level of constructive controversy. Used in this context, controversy is defined as the willingness to explore *all* sides of every issue. Thus achieving controversy is a desired goal, not something to avoid. How does one build constructive controversy into the team? Following are some of the key ingredients:

1. *Common goals or vision.* If diverse people can all commit themselves to a common set of goals or a shared vision as to what they can accomplish together, they may be able to combine their richness of difference in new and more innovative ways. Thus teams characterized by diversity must spend time coming to agreements as to what they want to accomplish together.

2. *Diversity as a value.* Team members must understand and accept as a shared value that diversity of background and experience is a positive ingredient. They need to discuss what controversy is and see controversy as the willingness to explore all facets of all issues before any decisions or plans are concluded. People on the team might describe their own differences so others can understand "where they are coming from" when they express ideas and opinions.

3. *Guidelines for work.* Assuming that members of the diverse team have developed a commitment to common goals and accept diversity as a value, developing a set of guidelines for work is immensely useful. Even a

---

[9]For a discussion of diversity and innovation in organizations, see D. Tjosvold, *Team Organization* (New York: Wiley, 1991), especially Chapter 10. See also Tjosvold's book *The Conflict-Positive Organization: Stimulate Diversity and Create Unity* (Reading, Mass.: Addison-Wesley, 1991).

diverse group will have deadlines to meet and accomplishments that need to be presented. The following guidelines might be helpful:

a. Every team member who has some experience with an issue is expected to share his or her own best thinking on that issue.

b. If one agrees or disagrees with another member, one should share that position with the group.

c. The team might adopt the Golden Rule of diverse communications: Discuss issues with others as you would like them to discuss them with you, and listen to others as you would like them to listen to you.

d. Before any decision is finalized, the leader or a group member should ask, "Have we heard every idea, suggestion, or argument about this proposal?"

e. Any person who disagrees with another should be able to repeat back to the first person's satisfaction the other's position to make sure that one disagrees with what the person meant, not what was heard.

f. It should be completely accepted that every member of the team is a person of worth and intelligence and that therefore every person's opinions, ideas, and arguments should be listened to with respect.

g. The following might be a team slogan: Controversy, when discussed in a cooperative context, promotes elaboration of views, the search for new information and ideas, and the integration of apparently opposing positions.

4. *Critiquing.* Every team, especially a diverse team, should take the time to critique its own processes and performance. How well has the team followed its own guidelines? What has hindered us from being as creative as possible? Have we used controversy constructively? What do we need to do to become a more effective team and use our diversity more productively?

This chapter has explored two ends of a team continuum. On the one end is the team paralyzed by fear, willing to make decisions that no one personally thinks are useful. The other end is the truly diverse team that has the danger of bogging down or splitting up because it may be too open and stand on members' differences rather than using controversy constructively. Both types are challenges, and teams at both ends can be found even in the same organization. It is the hope and the challenge that with courage, sensitivity, and shared planning and participation, these difficulties can be managed.

# 6

# Team Development Through Leadership Training

Many managers and supervisors have worked with the same group of people in primarily staff-boss relationships but need to turn their staffs into real teams. The process starts by training team leaders in the knowledge and skills they need to guide staff people in the transition to effective team members. Team-leadership training is an important way of ensuring that teamwork is developed in the organization. If a leader knows how to develop a team, the skill follows the leader. This chapter combines the issues involved in turning a staff into a team with identifying those elements needed in a team-leadership training program.[1]

A staff differs from a team in a number of significant ways. Since managing the transition from a staff to a team is a condition facing many team leaders, they must first understand these differences (see Table 6.1).

## The Shift from Management to Leadership

It is clear that a critical difference between a staff and a team is the power and role of the "boss." In a staff the superior is traditionally in charge, and staff members are seen primarily as workers to carry out the assignments or actions decreed by the superior. A team still has a recognized leader, but that person's use of power and definition of the role are very different. The team's leader tends to give more responsibility to the team, opens

---

[1]Much of this chapter is based on the work of Dr. Robert Dyer.

**Table 6.1**
*Differences Between a Staff and a Team*

| Characteristic | A Staff | A Team |
|---|---|---|
| • Goals and decisions | Made by the boss | Made jointly by team and boss |
| • Assignments | Made by the boss | Made jointly by the boss and subordinates |
| • Communications | In a meeting are primarily between the boss and a subordinate | Are open among all team members |
| • Role of subordinate | Primarily to carry out assignments | Team members initiate action, make suggestions, and help in planning |
| • Primary virtues | Loyalty and being a "good soldier" | Trust, helping, and creativity |
| • Sharing of data | Data shared on basis of what people feel the boss wants | All relevant data shared |
| • Critical feedback | Rare and anxiety provoking | Regarded as important to improvement |
| • Differences and conflicts | Avoided or smoothed over | Regarded as enriching; worked through |
| • Work | Each staff person responsible for own work | Team members feel responsible for one another |
| • Goal | Boss's primary goal is to get the job done | Team leader works to get results and develop team members |

up lines of communication, encourages collaboration and mutual helping among members, and allows—even encourages—differences and works through them. The leader spends time building the team so that team members feel responsible for working together to accomplish common goals.

In order to achieve this shift from a staff to a team, a first objective is to help the boss shift more power and responsibility to team members and to redefine that role. Figure 6.1 shows what this shift in power and role needs to be to change a staff, or any imn.ature team, into a real team.

In the beginning of the shift from staff to team, the superior is usually in a traditional role. Authority is deposited primarily in this person, and a minimal amount of real power or authority is delegated to subordinates. The power person must be helped (trained, oriented, educated) to see the leadership role in an effective team in a radically different way. The boss who is to become a leader must experience a true paradigm shift in order for the development of the team to take place.

**Figure 6.1**
*Team-Development Model*

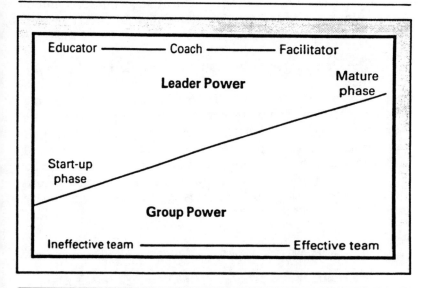

In the classic Blake-Mouton Managerial Grid five modal management styles are identified.[2] The basic philosophy and primary goal of the 9/1 manager is achieving results, output, or production. In this style managers are responsible for seeing that work is accomplished, and any means could be seen as appropriate to achieving this overriding goal. To a 1/9 manager, by contrast, the pivotal concern is ensuring that the needs of people are met. The philosophy underlying this style is that in order to be productive, workers must be happy. Thus the manager's job is to keep workers' morale high. Contrary to this notion, for years Fred Herzberg conducted research to show that morale is a function of the nature of the task itself, not a result of "hygiene" behaviors of the boss.[3]

To managers with a 1/1 orientation, people should be left alone to "do their own thing." These *laissez-faire* managers might paraphrase the old adage about government, that style of government is best which governs least, and assert: That management manages best that manages least. A very different stance is adopted by the 5/5 manager, who takes total responsibility for work results and the needs of people. The philosophy of this completely dedicated superior is: I am the one who must see that all things are done to move the work ahead. If goals are not met, I am responsible, and I must work harder. Using this spectrum of managerial styles, Blake and Mouton found in their research that a preponderance of organizations and managers fit the 5/5 style.

The 9/9 manager, however, has a very different philosophy about the role of the manager, and it is this paradigm shift that becomes a fundamental matter in training managers to become true team leaders. To this type of manager, all members of the team must be equally committed to accomplishing the goals and being committed to helping one another. The leader's central task is to build the team. With this orientation, the way the team leader spends his or her time, interacts with subordinates, conducts meetings, sets goals, and makes decisions is very different from what takes place under other styles.

---

[2]R. R. Blake and J. S. Mouton, *The Managerial Grid* (Houston: Gulf, 1964).

[3]F. Herzberg, *Work and the Nature of Man* (Cleveland: World Publishing, 1966).

One of the basic problems that organizations face in achieving this paradigm shift among middle- and lower-level managers and supervisors is that the management style ingrained in the organization's culture and the preferred style of top management may be one of "tough results" management and not true team leadership. Although these top managers may verbalize the importance of teams, their own style may well belie their statements. Furthermore, these managers often tend to reward and promote those whose style is similar to theirs.

A true paradigm shift occurs most easily if the behavior of power people from the top down is consistent with a team philosophy, team leadership is discussed openly at all levels, clear role models of good leadership behavior exist in the organization, and people are rewarded for engaging in effective team development. Closely connected to the notion of a philosophy of leadership or management and a paradigm shift is the clear message from much current research on leadership, namely, that the leader with the most impact has a clear vision as to what and how goals are to be achieved and can communicate this vision to others. This vision should include a commitment to building teams through which people accomplish goals as they work collaboratively.

## New Leadership Roles

### *Leader as Educator*

Assuming that the leader is committed to being a true team leader, the first task is to educate the team members as to the dimensions of real teamwork. How does the team leader learn about the demands of the role of the team leader? This is probably best done in a training program for current and potential team leaders. Such a program would discuss the philosophy of team leadership and present research on the value of participation, collaboration, and teamwork. Participants would go through exercises demonstrating teamwork and the role of the team leader. Each phase of moving from an immature to a mature team needs to be presented, discussed, and practiced.

Following the training program, the team leader can, ideally, begin to educate the team members on the key characteristics of a team and the important roles of the team members and

the leader. If the leader feels inadequate to conduct these education sessions, an outside facilitator could be used to help in the
education of the team but not in running the team meetings.

In this education phase the leader as educator develops
the following changes: (1) a willingness to share power and responsibility with team members, (2) encouragement of team
members to become more active in sharing leadership responsibilities, (3) development with team members of the basic characteristics of an effective team and acceptance of them as goals,
(4) development of new guidelines on how the team will function
in the future, and (5) presentation and practice of the key skills
of team members: being trusting and trustworthy, fostering open
communications (sharing all relevant data), giving and receiving
feedback, making decisions that have the commitment of all, and
observing and critiquing group processes.

*1. Sharing Power.*   It is by sharing power that the
team leader shows commitment to the new paradigm or philosophy of management. This can be done in a variety of ways: asking a team member to build a team meeting agenda by contacting
each team member for agenda items; allowing a team member to
chair a team meeting; asking team members for their ideas, suggestions, or criticisms of proposals on the table; setting goals and
making decisions that involve full participation; or delegating
significant work to team members without continually checking
up on them.

Sharing power is the basis of true participative management. Team members must feel that they are partners with the
team leader in the work to be done, that their ideas are listened
to and respected, and that they can disagree with the team
leader without fear of reprisal.

*2. Sharing Leadership.*   The concept here to be taught
and practiced is that leadership is not something deposited in a
position but is instead a process that can be shared with others.
A person who shares in the leadership process sees an action that
is needed to move the team ahead and then takes initiative to
take the action. Leadership is truly shared when every team
member tries as much as possible to initiate an action whenever
he or she sees the team struggling or getting bogged down. Team
members do not sit and say to themselves, "If the leader doesn't

do something soon, we are going to waste a lot of time and make some very poor decisions."

**3.** *Understanding the Characteristics of an Effective Team.* These characteristics should be generated by the team members in a team meeting. The team leader asks, "If we are to become a truly effective team, what would we look like? Let us spend some time now identifying what we think are the important characteristics of an effective team." With the team leader participating but not dominating, the team members develop their list. (A list of characteristics is given in Chapter 2. The team can compare its list with the one in this book.)

The team leader could also ask, "For which of these characteristics do we have some strength, and which ones do we need to work on?" This is an important first discussion leading to building a team. The discussion should lead to some kind of action needed by both team members and the leader to become more effective in the areas identified.

**4.** *Developing Team Guidelines.* Next, what guidelines does the team need to become effective according to its own criteria and to avoid pitfalls? Again with the leader participating but not dominating, the team develops its own set of guidelines. The leader might say, "We need guidelines that would promote open discussion, on how we will make decisions, and on how we will deal with disagreements among team members. We need guidelines on how to ensure that people follow through on assignments." (See also the guidelines suggested in Chapter 11.)

These guidelines should be agreed on by all team members and should be written up and posted for display at all team meetings. Periodically the team should stop and consider whether it is following its own guidelines and whether any guidelines need to be added or changed.

**5.** *Identifying Key Member Skills.* In this educative phase members should discuss and practice skills that seem to be imperative if the team is to develop. One is *trust behavior*—trusting and being trustworthy. The fundamental emotional condition in a team is not liking but trusting. People do not need to like one another as friends to be able to work together, but they do need to trust one another. Thus each team member must be both trustworthy and trusting of others, assuming that they are also trustworthy. Being trustworthy means keeping confidences, carrying out assignments, supporting others when they need support, giving both honest positive feedback and helpful critical feedback, being present at team meetings, and being available to team members.

If the trust level has been low in the relationships as a staff, this issue needs to be aired in the team meeting. Trust would be increased if the aspects of trust were identified and all team members verbally committed themselves to being trustworthy and trusting others. Some teams have developed a guideline for amnesty; team members will grant amnesty for all past behaviors and will respond only to current and future behaviors of others they may have previously distrusted. The amnesty guideline further indicates that a team member who feels that another has behaved in a nontrustworthy way will go to the other and say, "I could be wrong, but I have felt that you were not as trustworthy as I thought was appropriate. Could we talk about this?" Such an encounter is sensitive and delicate, and the hope is that the matter could be discussed without either party becoming defensive or belligerent. Sometimes it is helpful to have a third party present to mediate this discussion.

Another needed skill is *open communications*. This involves some risk if the norm in the staff has been to keep quiet and say only what you think the boss wants to hear. It is helpful if the team leader, consistent with the new team philosophy, can say, "I honestly want every person to speak up and share his or her thinking, regardless of whether it is in agreement." As part of the educative phase it is sometimes helpful for the leader to initiate a team-oriented exercise (Desert Survival, Arctic Survival, and so on) so that the team has a chance to practice being open, making decisions, testing out the trust level, and observing the leader's behavior. The team then has an opportunity to critique its performance after the conclusion of the exercise. In the training, team leaders should be introduced to various exercises to give them some experience in how to administer and use the games.

A natural extension of open communications is *giving and receiving feedback*. Some guidelines of effective feedback should be discussed. For example, feedback is best given if it is asked for rather than unsolicited. Feedback is more easily accepted if given in the form of a suggestion, as, for example, "I think you would be more effective if you asked a number of people for their ideas rather than just one or two." This is easier feedback to hear than evaluative feedback, such as, "I think you play favorites and listen only to people you like." Feedback is also positive, and people need to hear what they do well just as much as what they need to improve.

Sometimes feedback needs to be shared in the team setting if, for example, a person's behavior is blocking the group. Sometimes, however, it is best if the feedback is solicited and given in a one-on-one situation. If a person giving feedback feels uncertain, it can be useful to express the dilemma: "John, I have a dilemma. I have some feedback I think would be useful to you, but I am reluctant to share it with you for fear it might disrupt our relationship. I value our relationship and it is more important than giving the feedback. How do you think I should deal with this dilemma?" Given this context, the person usually will ask for the feedback to be shared.

*Making decisions that have commitment* is another key skill. Teams must make a wide range of decisions—about goals, programs, use of resources, assignments, schedules, and so forth. It should be made clear that in an effective team, not all decisions are made by consensus (all team members agree that the decision made is one they understand and can implement, not necessarily their first choice). As Vroom's work on decision making shows, sometimes the team leader should appropriately make authoritative decisions, sometimes should consult with team members before making a decision, and sometimes should make group-consensus decisions.[4] The mode of decision making used depends on how critical the decision is, whether the leader has all the data, and whether the team's commitment will be affected by an authoritative decision.

These various decision modes need to be discussed, the key decisions identified, and agreement reached on the decision style to be used. A team exercise on decision making is very useful for practicing decision-making skills in this phase of team development.

Most organizational team members are not going to become skilled group observers or facilitators. But they can become

---

[4] V. H. Vroom and P. W. Yetton, *Leadership and Decision Making* (Pittsburgh: University of Pittsburgh Press, 1973).

skilled at observing and critiquing group processes. They can build in a structure that will allow them to deal with most problems that occur as a team works together. This structure includes setting a time for the team to stop and critique how it has been functioning. It is not that difficult to save some time at the end of a team meeting and then ask, What did we do in this meeting that allowed us to be productive? What did we do in this meeting that bogged us down or decreased our effectiveness? What do we need to do to improve our effectiveness in our team meetings?

It is useful if the team can understand that all groups function at two levels: (1) the task level, where people are trying to make decisions and get work done, and (2) a relationship level, where people are dealing with one another's feelings and ongoing relationships. At the task level teams need people to give ideas and suggestions, evaluate ideas, make decisions and assignments, and allocate resources. At the relationship level team members need to support and encourage one another, invite more hesitant members to contribute, ease tension and provide some humor (without disrupting the task), and generally provide group maintenance, just as one would engage in maintenance of a piece of machinery.

Team members should understand and practice looking at those actions that block the team at either of these two levels and at least be able to say, "I feel uncomfortable now. I think we are bogged down and need to move ahead on our work" or "I think we have lost the participation of two members, and I would like to stop and see how they are feeling about what we are doing." Such actions could occur during the team meeting or might be shared during the critiquing session at the end.

It should be apparent that in the team-leadership training session, all of these concepts, with an opportunity to practice them, should be part of the training program. The goal is to prepare team leaders to conduct the education phase of the transition of a staff into a team or to be able to support a resource person who may be asked to handle this phase in collaboration with the team leader.

### Leader as Coach

About midway in the shift of power from leader to team, the leader has completed the education phase, and team members should now understand the new team orientation and have developed some competence in the new skills. Team members should also have experienced the willingness of the team leader to share responsibility and authority with them.

Now the leader enters into a new phase in the leader's role. The leader becomes a coach. Coaching is not a new concept in the field of management. Coaching means stopping work action at some needed point to identify for the team some mistake or disturbance in the way the team is functioning. As the coach, the leader may need to review the basic concept or the guidelines or may need to engage in some additional skill practice.

One of the mistakes a leader can make is to move too quickly up the power-shift line and start to coach when the team has not been adequately educated. If the leader starts to make decisions by consensus and the team members do not understand what consensus is, they could be confused by and suspicious of the leader's behavior. But if members understand what is happening in the team, coaching becomes a natural activity for the leader.

Sometimes coaching is best done for the whole team—reviewing again the guidelines of consensus or critiquing group processes. But sometimes coaching is most appropriate for a particular team member in a private session. In Chapter 12 the use of the Personal Management Interview (PMI) is discussed as a follow-up to team meetings, and in this private interview coaching can also be done productively.

### Leader as Facilitator

In this final phase in the transition from a staff to a team, the leader may function as a facilitator. Here the primary role of the leader is to intervene in the group's actions only when attention needs to be focused on a matter the team has not dealt with. Thus the leader as facilitator might say, "It seems to me that a vote is being taken before everyone has been able to speak. Do you see the same things I do?" Or the leader might intervene by saying, "If we move ahead in this direction, will this really get us to our overall mission or goals we have set? Have we reached a real or a false consensus? Does everyone feel satisfied with the way we have been functioning at this meeting?"

At this stage in the team's maturity the intervention of the leader at certain points is enough to get the team back on track, for members are now used to handling team actions themselves. However, it should not be assumed that the movement up the power line is fixed and one-way. It is quite possible that when new ideas, concepts, or skills are identified, the leader may need to shift back to the educator role or perhaps to the coaching role if some reminding or skill rehearsal is needed.

In the development of an effective team, the role of the leader is a critical variable.[5] The phases of the group's development and the training of the team leader have been discussed so that a training program for the development of the leader can be prepared. This process addresses one of the major problems of developing teams in organizations, namely, how to achieve the spread of the team effect in the total system. It is very time consuming and difficult to have a training staff or program for training each team separately. A better way is to devise an effective program for training team leaders so *they* can build a team wherever they are assigned. However, it is also very important that the entire management system support the team notion and that the reward system reward leaders who are effective. Otherwise, a team leader goes through the team-leadership training program but is not supported or rewarded appropriately in the formal reward system. This can almost ensure that the team-leadership program will not be applied in the organization.

## Measurement of Team Maturity

In addition to following a process for turning an immature group or staff into a mature team, an ongoing team can use a scale (Fig. 6.2) to examine its processes to see what level of maturity it has achieved. Members of the team should fill out the scale, compute an average for the total team, and identify the areas for which more team building is needed. One should think of this scale in connection with the model in Fig. 6.1. Think of the power line in the middle of the model in Fig. 6.1 as representing a scale from 1 (start-up team or immature team) to 5 (a mature team), with 3 being the midpoint.

---

[5]For another view of the role of the leader in a new team see Larry Hirschhorn, *Managing in the New Team Environment: Skills, Tools, and Methods* (Reading, Mass.: Addison-Wesley, 1991).

**Figure 6.2**
*Team-Maturity Scale*

Based on your observations of your work unit, evaluate the maturity of your group as a mature team.

**1 How are goals established in your work unit?**

| 1 | 2 | 3 | 4 | 5 |
|---|---|---|---|---|
| The group leader sets the goals for us. | | We discuss goals, but finally the leader sets the goals. | | We all work together to arrive at our goals. |

**2. How committed are the people in your unit to working hard to achieve the goals?**

| 1 | 2 | 3 | 4 | 5 |
|---|---|---|---|---|
| People demonstrate surface-level commitment to the goals. | | People work at achieving the goals with which they agree. | | Everyone is deeply committed to all of the goals. |

**3. How are decisions made in your unit?**

| 1 | 2 | 3 | 4 | 5 |
|---|---|---|---|---|
| The boss tells us what the decisions are. | | We discuss issues, but the boss makes all final decisions. | | We all make appropriate decisions by consensus. |

*(continued)*

**Figure 6.2** *(continued)*

**4. How well do people collaborate with others?**

| 1 | 2 | 3 | 4 | 5 |
|---|---|---|---|---|
| Each person works independent of others. | | There is some collaboration when people are pushed to it. | | People easily work with others as needed. |

**5. How much do people trust each other—to carry out assignments, to keep confidences, to do their share, to help when needed?**

| 1 | 2 | 3 | 4 | 5 |
|---|---|---|---|---|
| There is almost no trust at all. | | Some trust exists, but it is not widespread. | | There is high trust among all. |

**6. How would you describe the unit leader's management style?**

| 1 | 2 | 3 | 4 | 5 |
|---|---|---|---|---|
| S/he is authoritarian—runs things his/her way. | | S/he is consultative—consults with us, but has final say. | | S/he is participative—is part of the team. |

**7. How open and free are communications in unit meetings?**

| 1 | 2 | 3 | 4 | 5 |
|---|---|---|---|---|
| Communication is very closed, guarded, and careful. | | People will talk about matters that are safe. | | Everyone feels free to say what they want. |

**8. When people have differences or conflicts, how are they handled?**

| 1 | 2 | 3 | 4 | 5 |
|---|---|---|---|---|
| Conflicts are ignored, or people are told not to worry about them. | | Conflicts are sometimes looked at but are usually left hanging. | | Conflicts are discussed openly and resolved. |

**9. What is the level of people feeling they are part of a team?**

| 1 | 2 | 3 | 4 | 5 |
|---|---|---|---|---|
| People really don't feel like they are part of a team. | | Occasionally, there is a sense of team spirit. | | There is a deep feeling of team pride and spirit. |

*(continued)*

**Figure 6.2** *(continued)*

**10. To what extent do people in your work unit understand what people need from each other in order to achieve common goals?**

| 1 | 2 | 3 | 4 | 5 |
|---|---|---|---|---|
| People really don't understand what others need from them. | | There is some understanding between some people. | | Each person truly understands what others need from him/her. |

**11. To what extent do people really understand, accept, and implement decisions and assignments with commitments?**

| 1 | 2 | 3 | 4 | 5 |
|---|---|---|---|---|
| People just do what they are told. There is little personal commitment. | | At times there is some commitment to decisions and assignments; at other times there is not. | | There is full commitment by everyone to all decisions and assignments. |

**12. How supportive and helpful are the unit leaders and members toward one another?**

| 1 | 2 | 3 | 4 | 5 |
|---|---|---|---|---|
| There is little support among leaders and members. | | There is some support and help some of the time. | | There is high support and help most of the time. |

**13. Does your work unit ever stop and critique how well they are working together?**

| 1 | 2 | 3 | 4 | 5 |
|---|---|---|---|---|
| We never stop to critique how well we are doing. | | We occasionally take time to critique how well we are doing. | | We regularly take time to critique how well we are doing. |

**14. Generally how satisfied are you with the way your work unit functions as a team?**

| 1 | 2 | 3 | 4 | 5 |
|---|---|---|---|---|
| I am not satisfied at all. | | Sometimes I'm satisfied; sometimes not. | | I am very satisfied almost all of the time. |

**15. To what extent is the work unit dependent on the unit leader to move ahead and get work done?**

| 1 | 2 | 3 | 4 | 5 |
|---|---|---|---|---|
| Completely dependent on the leader. | | Somewhat dependent. | | Able to work independently as needed. |

**16. Is your unit leader capable of building your group into an effective team?**

| 1 | 2 | 3 | 4 | 5 |
|---|---|---|---|---|
| Not capable at all. | | Somewhat capable. | | Completely capable. |

*(continued)*

**Figure 6.2** *(continued)*

**17. Do group members in your work unit have the knowledge and skills necessary to build an effective team?**

| 1 | 2 | 3 | 4 | 5 |
|---|---|---|---|---|
| Skills and knowledge are not there. | | Some people have skills and knowledge. | | Members have adequate skills and knowledge. |

**18. Are people willing to take a risk and try out new actions to make the team better?**

| 1 | 2 | 3 | 4 | 5 |
|---|---|---|---|---|
| No one is willing to risk. | | Some willingness to risk. | | High willingness to risk. |

**19. Group members are willing to make personal sacrifices for the good of the team.**

| 1 | 2 | 3 | 4 | 5 |
|---|---|---|---|---|
| Almost never | | Sometimes | | Almost always |

**20. People feel they know how their work contributes to the goals of the total group.**

| 1 | 2 | 3 | 4 | 5 |
|---|---|---|---|---|
| No real understanding | | Some understanding | | Complete understanding |

**21. Team members know how to get work done and maintain good relationships at the same time.**

| 1 | 2 | 3 | 4 | 5 |
|---|---|---|---|---|
| Don't do this well | | Have some ability | | Completely able to do this |

**22. Team members are sensitive to the needs of other members of the team.**

| 1 | 2 | 3 | 4 | 5 |
|---|---|---|---|---|
| No sensitivity | | Some sensitivity | | Complete sensitivity |

**Scoring:** Each person should add up his or her score for the twenty-two items and divide that total by 22. This will give the perceived maturity score of the team. If you add up all of the individual scores and divide by the number of members of the team, you will find the team's rating of its maturity. If the ratings are 3.75 or higher, there is evidence that there is an appropriate level of maturity. If the scores are between 2.5 and 3.75, this indicates that maturity is at a midlevel, and there is still work to be done by the team and team leader. If the score is between 1.00 and 2.50, the indications are that the team is at an immature level, and a great deal of team building is needed.

An item analysis, looking at the individual and team scores for each item, will help the team see the areas that need the most work to move the team to a higher level of maturity.

*This scale used with Permission of Novations, Inc. Provo, Utah.

# 7

# Building the Total Collaborative Team Organization

This chapter asserts that building effective work teams in organizations will not be successful until and unless the total organization is seen as being committed to a collaborative, team-oriented way of life. This means that management at all levels must understand and behave collaboratively. The organization's culture and systems must be in congruence, and individuals must have the knowledge and skills necessary to function in a team mode.

## Dimensions of Collaborative Organizations

Much of the research and writing on the human factors in organizations over the past three decades clearly points out that there are three component forces that seriously affect human performance in the organization (see Fig. 7.1). These three components—culture, systems, and individuals—form a triangle. Unless teamwork and collaboration are part of the organization's culture, the organization's systems, and the individual's arsenal of skill and knowledge, the organization will probably be unable to sustain a process of high involvement and participation at all levels in the organization.

### Culture

This is the broadest area of organizational influence. This component is the most powerful, is often the most difficult to detect, and is the most difficult to change. An organization's culture represents the basic shared values and assumptions held by most

**Figure 7.1**
*Components of the Collaborative Organization*

people in the organization. Culture defines what things are right or wrong, what matters are important, how one gets into trouble, and how people are expected to see the whole corporate world.

It is critical to the collaborative team organization that the shared culture emphasize that teamwork is essential and that people at all levels get into trouble if they do not collaborate with others and respond readily as a member of the total team. If the culture is either openly or passively resistant to the importance of teamwork, any attempts to foster collaboration or participation or involvement will be seen as either a temporary action or a management manipulation.

### Systems

All organizations function on the basis of agreed-on methods for doing work in the organization. These integrated agreements, or systems, regulate almost all aspects of organization life. Thus pay systems, evaluation and promotion systems, decision-making systems, and management systems are all examples of this component.

It is critical that the systemic aspects of the organization be in agreement with the broader, shared cultural orientations. People encounter major problems in a company that is attempting to build teamwork into the bedrock culture, when the pay system, for example, is based entirely on individual performance. The organization's culture and its systems must be congruent.

## Individuals

Inside the fabric of the culture and the systems of the organization are the workers, ranging from top-level managers or administrators with broad power and influence down to the hourly workers, who usually are the ones producing the product or service. Most organizations spend considerable time orienting their workers to the demands of the culture and the systems. However, if workers are to function effectively and consistently with the most popular aspects of the culture or the systems, they must have appropriate knowledge and skills. If workers do not know what they are to do or how they are to behave or what skills they need to be competent, the influence of the culture or the systems is minimized.

On the other hand, it has been observed that much organizational change has centered on training—management or employee training. But if the knowledge and skills expected in the training activities are not rewarded in the systems or are at variance with what people understand the culture to be, the impact of training is severely reduced. Hence culture, systems, and individual performance must all be consistent with one another if the organization is to be truly collaborative over time.

## Culture and System Congruence

General Motors, like most companies recently, has spent considerable time fine-tuning its statement of corporate values, or mission statement. GM boldly asserts that its values include "People, Teamwork, Continuous Improvement, and Customer Satisfaction."[1] Does such a written statement have a significant impact on the behavior of employees in the organization? Schlesinger and Ingrassie, in their *Wall Street Journal* article, point out that GM chairman Roger Smith sent a first-ever year-end thank-you letter stating, "We value you as members of the GM family and our team. Sometimes we may not express this feeling very well. We will try to do better." Although GM executives said that this was the beginning of a cultural revolution, many employees were cynical and skeptical, suspecting that it was "all silliness born of desperation." "The only thing different is that they're smoother," said Dave Yettaw, the president of UAW local 599 at the Buick City complex in Flint, Michigan. The foreman used to say, "Do it because I'm the boss. Now he puts his arm around you and says, "Listen, John, let's have a coffee. How have you been doing? How's your dog? Did your daughter win her baton championship? Look, we've got this problem."[2]

The critical issue for GM and for many organizations trying to change the organization's culture from a top-down, authoritarian posture to a more collaborative, teamwork condition is, What must be done to make a fundamental change in the culture of the organization? All organizations are a complex mixture of both cultural and system conditions. Culture represents the physical artifacts and the basic beliefs that direct the thinking, feelings, perceptions, and behaviors of the people in the culture. The system aspects of the organization are the integrated structures and processes that allow the organization to function and accomplish its goals.

The great dilemma facing many organizations is that they want to change the culture—that is, foster a belief that people and teamwork are truly valued—but they want to keep system conditions unaltered. The basic systemic processes—performance review, evaluation, pay, and promotion—stay the same. When system processes are at variance with an espoused cultural value, members of the organization are legitimately confused and skeptical. They want to see the espoused culture put into practice, and that comes only when system conditions also change and there is congruence at both the cultural and system levels.

### Incongruence in the Organization

As Frampton has written:

> CEOs say "We're a team, we're all in this together, rah, rah, rah." But the employees look at the difference between their pay and the CEOs'. They see top management's perks—oak dining rooms and heated garages, vs. cafeterias for the hourly guys and parking spaces half a

---

[2]*Ibid.*

mile from the plant. And they wonder: "Is this together-
ness?" As the disparity in pay widens, the wonder grows.[3]

Communication gaps also appear when there is no congruence between values and systems. Exxon says that people are
their most important resource, yet when they went through a
major restructuring in 1986, which meant reducing the work-
force as much as 30 percent in some units, the majority of Exxon
employees learned of this major downsizing by reading it first in
the *Wall Street Journal.*

Management often feels that it is sending out crucial information, but down in the ranks people feel that they are not getting the word. In a survey done by the Forum Corp., a consulting
firm, 82 percent of Fortune 500 executives believe that their corporate strategy is understood by everyone who needs to know.
But Louis Harris research finds that fewer than one-third of employees say that management provides clear goals and directions. When asked what workers wanted more from top
management, people said, "reliable information on where the
company is headed" and "how my job fits into the total."[4]

### Culture and System Analysis

The latest thinking on organizational culture indicates that four
elements exist. They range from those factors that are most evident and least important to those that are least evident but
vital.[5]

1. *Artifacts*—the tangible aspects of the culture. Logos,
   employee dress, office layouts, titles, washroom keys,
   and parking spaces are all artifacts of the culture.

2. *Perspectives*—shared ideas and actions that help people act appropriately in handling performance reviews,
   making a presentation to the management committee
   (always using slides or overheads), addressing a superior appropriately, or other situations.

[3]W. Frampton, "The Trust Gap," *Fortune*, May 1989:53–59.

[4]Frampton, *Op. cit.,* p. 58.

[5]See E. H. Schein, *Organizational Culture and Leadership. Second
Edition* (San Francisco: Jossey-Bass, 1992) for a more detailed discussion of culture.

3. *Values*—the general ideals, standards, and "sins" in the organization. The organization may say that it values its human resources, honesty, and integrity; protects the environment; promotes from within; and listens to the customer. These values are often stated in the corporate mission statement or philosophy.

4. *Basic assumptions*—the core of culture—the bedrock beliefs that people in the culture hold about themselves, other people, and the world. In some organizations the basic assumptions include profit as the name of the game, the good employee as good soldier, or the need to keep one's mouth shut and not make waves. In another culture the beliefs might focus on the need to be aggressive and take risks to get ahead, and on the notions that people want to be treated fairly and that management is paid to make decisions.

The old dichotomy of McGregor's Theory X and Y represents two contrasting basic assumptions.[6] Theory X assumes that people are basically lazy and need to be controlled. Theory Y assumes that people want to work and make contributions. Thus if an organization holding to the basic assumptions that people need to be controlled and that management is paid to make decisions then makes an artifact change, adopting a new logo or slogan or even a value statement that "we value people," employees will react with cynicism.

### System Analysis

Despite a myriad of connected system parts in an organization, there are three major subsystems, as follows:

1. *The social system*—the defined ways that people are to work, decide, communicate, help, and solve problems. This subsystem includes the emotional climate, status and role relationships, the decision-making process, and the selection and use of people.

2. *The technical or operation system*—the method for getting work done, including the unique arrangements of equipment, material, space, and work-flow processes.

---

[6]D. McGregor, *The Human Side of Enterprise* (New York: McGraw-Hill, 1960) and W. G. Dyer, *Strategies for Managing Change* (Reading, Mass.: Addison-Wesley, 1984), Chapter 3.

3. *The administrative or management system*—the standards, rules, and regulations that direct the other two subsystems. This subsystem includes wage and salary processes, hiring and firing, promotions, benefits, budgets, and priorities.

This chapter suggests that unless the basic assumptions and values in the organization's culture are reflected in one or more of the primary subsystems, congruence will be lacking in the organization, and people will doubt any programs to build a collaborative or teamwork process.

## The Individual in the Organization

We have examined the connection between the culture and the systems, but how do individuals in the organization handle their own performance? For years various attempts have been made to increase the productivity or effectiveness of people in organizations. Such attempts include management training, the use of incentives, bonuses, flextime, MBO, and others.

The research on training has shown for years that people who go away to a training program may in fact make some changes during or just after the training. But when they return home, they revert to the old behaviors. Why? Clearly the new behaviors suggested in the training are not rewarded by the organization's systems or may be contrary to the existing values and basic assumptions of the culture.

Motivation theory outlines some of the factors that need to be present if people are "motivated" to improve performance. Victor Vroom developed a useful motivation model called *expectation theory*.[7] According to this model, people evaluate their total situation and think about both the outcomes or results that are desirable to them and what they can realistically expect in the organization. They then examine what they regard as the appropriate strategies available that can be expected to achieve the desired outcome. In other words, we have expected outcomes and expected strategies to achieve the desired results. If a person desires a promotion and expects that extra hours and extra work are required to get that promotion, he or she will be "motivated" to do the extra things to produce the desired outcome. However, if in the particu-

---

[7]V. H. Vroom, *Work and Motivation* (New York: Wiley, 1964).

lar culture the strategy that one thinks (expects) will work is to get the political support of a strong figure, political maneuvering will be used. Individual performance cannot be seen as something separate from the culture and systems of the organization.

However, suppose that a significant attempt is made to bring the culture and systems in line with an honest emphasis on teamwork and collaboration. How does a first-line supervisor who has never experienced real teamwork before suddenly begin to manage a team effectively? Similarly, how do workers who have always been treated as cogs in a machine learn to accept responsibility as team members? At this point it is important that people in the organization at all levels be given adequate orientation or socialization to the culture and systems. They would also need training that would allow them to feel competent to behave in new, collaborative ways. Thus training and individual development or group skill development for team members is a necessary part of building the collaborative, team-oriented organization.

## Bringing the Organization into Balance

An organization is in balance when all three critical dimensions are in congruence. Such a change program is most complex.

### Changes in Culture

Bringing about change in the culture is probably the most difficult goal in all change efforts. One of the key factors is that any culture change must be supported, if not initiated, by the key power people. Some researchers have suggested that a rather isolated, highly autonomous unit of an organization can achieve some real culture change, which can be then held up by the power people as an example of what can be achieved. But the example will not spread widely without top-management support.

Another critical factor is the congruence between the espoused culture and the culture in practice. The espoused culture is what is presented as the "ideal"—what the organization says it believes in. Often these ideal assumptions and values are represented in the company's goals, mission statements, or stated values. These ideals must then be translated into action and become the culture in practice. When there is any significant divergence between what the organization says it believes in and what various stakeholders experience as the culture in practice, a cynicism gap is created, and the trust level drops significantly.

Bringing these two aspects of culture into balance is not easy. Some analysis must be made to ascertain both the espoused culture and the culture in practice. Top management must then look at any disparities and adopt a long-term commitment to put its ideals into practice. If the ideal is that "people are our most important resource," management at all levels must behave accordingly. They must listen to the people, respond to their input, give them recognition and responsibility, allow them to develop new competencies, and in general make the organization a rewarding and growthful experience for the employees. If the ideal is teamwork, managers at all levels of the organization must function in their work units as teams and not as staffs.

### Changes in Systems

A complete review must be made of all formal systems, especially the reward, evaluation, promotion, performance review, management, and career-development systems. It is especially important that the various systems reflect the new cultural norms and values being put in place. If the culture says that it values creativity, the reward system must be directly connected, and the management system must be such that managers are encouraging and using creative input.

The whole new thrust in organization redesign means that the technical or operation system is going to be reviewed. Is the technical system well connected to the social system (sociotechnical system), and does this reflect the culture? It does not seem possible to redesign organizations and not understand the use of teams, and this whole movement must reflect the culture and the other systems.

### Changes in Individuals

If workers in the organization are to function effectively in the desired culture, they must have the knowledge and skills to perform well, and the reward systems must compensate people for their knowledge and skills. People get discouraged if they go through various training programs and then do not see the gains expected from the training reflected in the performance review process or the reward system or even appreciated by their superiors (part of the management system).

A human resource audit must be made to look at the kinds of people who will be needed for the long term. The recruitment and selection procedures need to be examined, as do the training and development programs that will be needed. All organizations are open systems, and we know that in the development of individuals the organization must look at the connections between a worker and that person's family, alternative opportunities, community values, influence of labor unions, and other organizations outside the company.

This open-system analysis is important in understanding both the forces that impact employees and those influences that will undoubtedly affect the culture and the systems. The totally effective collaborative organization cannot be created unless managers understand how to deal well with such external forces as government at all levels: special-interest groups, such as environmental groups, customers, suppliers, and competitors; economic conditions, external markets (especially internationally); and many other factors.

The organization world of the future will continue to be extremely complex, and it appears that those organizations that can create diverse, creative, effective teams will have the advantage. These organizations will work to keep the culture, systems, and individuals consistently congruent.

# Part II
# Alternative Team-Building Designs

# 8

# Preparing for Team Building

## Is Team Building Needed?

Usually a team-building program is undertaken when a concern, problem, issue, or set of symptoms leads the manager to believe that the effectiveness of the work unit is not up to par. The following major symptoms or conditions usually provoke serious thought or remedial action:

- Loss of production or unit output
- Increase of grievances or complaints from the staff
- Evidence of conflicts or hostility among staff members
- Confusion about assignments, missed signals, and unclear relationships
- Decisions misunderstood or not carried through properly
- Apathy and general lack of interest or involvement of staff members
- Lack of initiation, imagination, innovation—actions taken for solving complex problems
- Ineffective staff meetings, low participation, minimal effective decisions
- Slow start-up of a new group that needs to develop quickly into a working team
- High dependency on or negative reactions to the manager

- Complaints from users or customers about quality of service
- Continued unaccounted increase of costs

Most of these symptoms are *consequence* symptoms; that is, they result from or are caused by other factors. Loss of production, for example, is caused by such factors as conflicts between members or problems with one's boss. Two of the causal factors are especially important: (1) difficulty between team members and the team leader and (2) difficulty among team members.

### *Difficulty Between Team Members and the Team Leader*

Usually this symptom is obvious to the subordinates on the team and to an outside observer. Unfortunately, however, it may not be so apparent to the team leader. The problem is not that the leader and team members differ but rather how they deal with their differences. One common consequence of these differences is a condition of overconformity. Team members feel that the best way to get along with the team leader is just to go along with what they are told to do. They find that the easiest way to manage the relationship is to fall in line; doing so is less stressful than the alternative—ongoing conflict.

At times this conformance may represent true acceptance of the leader's position. A leader who is surrounded by people who are dependent thereby eliminates any possible conflict but also eliminates the richness of diverse opinion. Or the team members may have learned over time that conformity is the best strategy and may now automatically go along with whatever the leader suggests.

At other times conformity may represent passive resistance. People may agree with the leader publicly but privately resent and resist. Resistance may take subtle forms, such as losing decisions or never fully implementing them.

Another type of consequence is overt resistance—openly fighting or resisting what the leader wants. In this type of situation ordinary problem-solving procedures have been abandoned, and a struggle ensues whenever the leader gets together with team members. Or the struggle may go underground and although on the surface the interaction seems compatible, heavy infighting is going on behind the scenes.

Some superiors try to manage subordinates and the possibility of resistance by assuming a very strong authoritarian stance. The authoritarian leader demands obedience and uses a variety of control methods, both formal and informal, to influence behavior. People who are threatened by authority or who are used to high controls tend to become conforming. Those who do not accept authoritarian processes become resistant, either openly or under cover.

Other difficulties arise from a lack of trust. Team members may not trust the leader to give them honest information, represent them honestly, keep confidences, or carry through on promises. When trust is low, team members try to protect themselves. They are very guarded in what they say and are very suspicious of decisions and promises of action.

### Difficulty Among Team Members

This is one of the most widely observed symptoms of a sick team. These difficulties are described in different ways: people fight all of the time; they don't trust one another; there are personality conflicts; people have different philosophies, goals, or values. Usually the signals of team-member problems are strong statements of disagreement, with no attempt to reach agreements; complaints to the leader, indicating an unwillingness or inability to work out differences; avoidance of one another except when interaction is absolutely required; missed meetings or deadlines; work of poor quality; building of cliques or subgroups to protect against the other side; and minimal or very guarded communications.

It was differences in this area that originally led to the use of group methods to reveal problems among members and to learn to work through differences. Usually it is the manager who identifies one or more of the consequences or causal factors, although any unit member may share personal observations and diagnosis. Figure 8.1 is a checklist for identifying whether a team-development program is needed and whether a consultant is needed for such a program.

## Team Building as a Process

Team development should be thought of as an ongoing process, not as a single event. People who want to get away for a couple of days and "do team building" but then return to doing business as

**Figure 8.1**
*Team-Building Checklist*

**I. Problem Identification:** To what extent is there evidence of the following problems in your work unit?

| | Low Evidence | | Some Evidence | | High Evidence |
|---|---|---|---|---|---|
| 1. Loss of production or of work-unit output | 1 | 2 | 3 | 4 | 5 |
| 2. Grievances or complaints within the work unit | 1 | 2 | 3 | 4 | 5 |
| 3. Conflicts or hostility among unit members | 1 | 2 | 3 | 4 | 5 |
| 4. Confusion about assignments or unclear relationships between people | 1 | 2 | 3 | 4 | 5 |
| 5. Lack of clear goals or low commitment to goals | 1 | 2 | 3 | 4 | 5 |
| 6. Apathy or general lack of interest or involvement of unit members | 1 | 2 | 3 | 4 | 5 |

| | 1 | 2 | 3 | 4 | 5 |
|---|---|---|---|---|---|
| 7. Lack of innovation, risk taking, imagination, or taking initiative | 1 | 2 | 3 | 4 | 5 |
| 8. Ineffective staff meetings | 1 | 2 | 3 | 4 | 5 |
| 9. Problems in working with the boss | 1 | 2 | 3 | 4 | 5 |
| 10. Poor communications: people afraid to speak up, not listening to one another, or not talking together | 1 | 2 | 3 | 4 | 5 |
| 11. Lack of trust between leader and members or among members | 1 | 2 | 3 | 4 | 5 |
| 12. People do not understand or agree with decisions | 1 | 2 | 3 | 4 | 5 |
| 13. People feel that good work is not recognized or rewarded | 1 | 2 | 3 | 4 | 5 |

*(continued)*

**Table 8.1**   *(continued)*

| | 1 | 2 | 3 | 4 | 5 |
|---|---|---|---|---|---|
| 14. People are not encouraged to work together in better team effort | | | | | |

**Scoring:** Add up the score for the fourteen items. If your score is between 14 and 28, there is little evidence that your unit needs team building. If your score is between 29 and 42, there is some evidence, but no immediate pressure, unless two or three items are very high. If your score is between 43 and 56, you should seriously think about planning the team-building program. If your score is over 56, team building should be a top-priority item for your work unit.

**II.** Should you use an outside consultant to help in team building? (Circle the appropriate response.)

| | | | |
|---|---|---|---|
| 1. Does the manager feel comfortable in trying out something new and different with the staff? | Yes | No | ? |
| 2. Is the staff used to spending time in an outside location working on different issues of concern to the work unit? | Yes | No | ? |
| 3. Will group members speak up and give honest data? | Yes | No | ? |
| 4. Does your group generally work together without a lot of conflict or apathy? | Yes | No | ? |
| 5. Are you reasonably sure that the boss is not a major source of difficulty? | Yes | No | ? |

| | Yes | No | ? |
|---|---|---|---|
| 6. Is there a high commitment by the boss and unit members to achieve more effective team functioning ? | Yes | No | ? |
| 7. Is the personal style of the boss and his or her management philosophy consistent with a team approach? | Yes | No | ? |
| 8. Do you feel you know enough about team building to begin a program without help? | Yes | No | ? |
| 9. Would your staff feel confident enough to begin a team-building program without outside help? | Yes | No | ? |

**Scoring:** If you have circled six or more "yes" responses, you probably do not need an outside consultant. If you have four or more "no" responses, you probably do need a consultant. If you have a mixture of yes, no, and ? responses, you should probably invite in a consultant to talk over the situation and make a joint decision.

usual have an incorrect notion of the purpose of team building. The whole program is designed to alter the way an integrated unit functions together. This change is started at an initial meeting and continues through the next several months or years until the group learns to function as a team.

The team-development process often starts with a block of time devoted to helping the group look at its current level of team functioning and devising more effective ways of working together. This initial sequence of data sharing, diagnosis, and action planning takes time and should not be crammed into a couple of hours. Ideally, the members of the work group should plan to meet for at least one full day, and preferably two days, for the initial program. A common format is to meet for dinner, have an evening session, and then meet all the next day or for however long a time has been set aside.

Most team-building facilitators prefer to have a longer block of time (up to three days) to begin a team-development program. This may not be practical in some situations, and modifications must be made. Since we are thinking of team development as an ongoing process, it is possible to start with shorter amounts of time regularly scheduled over a period of several weeks. Some units have successfully conducted a program that opened with an evening meeting, followed by a two- to four-hour meeting each week for the next several weeks. Commitment to the process, regular attendance, high involvement, and good use of time are all more important than length of time.

It is customary to hold the initial team-development program away from the work site. The argument given is that if people meet at the work location, they will find it difficult to "turn off" their day-to-day concerns in order to concentrate fully on the goals of the program. This argument is compelling, even though there is little research evidence about the effect of the location on learning and change. Most practitioners do prefer to have development program at a location where they can have people's full time and attention.

### Use of a Consultant

Managers commonly ask, "Should I conduct the team development effort on my own, or should I get an outside person to help us?" "Outside person" could mean either a consultant from outside the organization or an internal consultant who is employed by the organization but is outside the work unit planning the team-development program. (Figure 8.1 includes a checklist for assessing the need for a consultant.)

Ultimately the manager should be responsible for the development of the work team. The consultant's job is to get the process started. The use of a consultant is generally advisable if a manager is aware of problems, feels that he or she may be one of the problems facing the work unit, and is not sure exactly what to do or how to do it but feels strongly enough that some positive action is necessary to pull the work group together for more effective operation.[1]

## *The Roles of the Manager and the Consultant*

Ultimately the development of a work team that can regularly stop and critique itself and plan for its improvement lies in the domain of management. It is the manager's responsibility to keep a finger on the pulse of his or her organization and to plan appropriate actions if the work unit shows signs of stress, ineffectiveness, or operating difficulty.

Unfortunately many managers have not yet been trained to do the data gathering, diagnosis, planning, and action taking required to maintain and improve their teams. The role of the consultant is to work with the manager until the manager is capable of incorporating team-development activities as a regular part of managerial responsibilities. The manager and the consultant (whether external or internal) should form their own two-person team in working through the initial team-building program. In all cases the manager will be responsible for all team-building activities, although he or she may use the consultant as a resource. The end result of the work of the consultant is to leave the manager capable of continuing team development without the assistance of the consultant or with minimum help.

---

[1] For a broader view of the role of the consultant, see Peter Block, *Flawless Consulting* (San Diego: Pfeiffer & Co., 1981) and E. H. Schein, *Process Consulting, Vol. 1: Its Role in Organization Development, Second Edition* (Reading, Mass.: Addison-Wesley, 1988).

### The Team-Building Cycle

Ordinarily a team-building program follows a cycle similar to that depicted in Fig. 8.2. The program begins because someone recognizes a problem or problems. Either before or during the team-building effort, data are gathered to determine the causes of the problem. The data are then analyzed, and a diagnosis is made of what is wrong and what is causing the problem. After the diagnosis, the work unit engages in appropriate planning and problem solving. Actions are planned and assignments made. The plans are then put into action and the results honestly evaluated.

Sometimes there is no clear, obvious problem that indicates the action. The concern is then to *identify* or find the problems that are present but hidden. One still gathers and analyzes the data, identifies the problems and the causes, and then moves to action planning. The manager and the consultant work together in carrying through the program from the time the problem has been identified through some form of evaluation.

**Figure 8.2**
*The Team-Building Cycle*

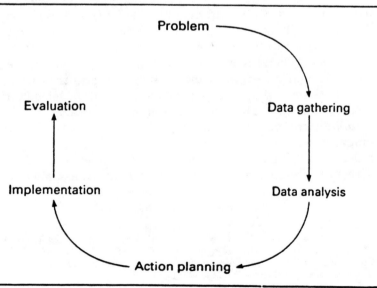

### Data Gathering

Since team development is essentially a program for training a staff to do its own problem solving and since a critical condition for effective problem solving is accurate data, a major concern of the manager-consultant team is to gather clear data on the causes behind the symptoms or problems originally identified. The consultant may initially assist in the data gathering, but eventually a team should develop the skill, so it can collect its own data as a basis for working on its own problems. Following are some common data-gathering devices.

*Interviews.* At times the consultant can perform a useful service by interviewing the members of the staff or unit. The consultant is trying to determine the factors behind the problem(s) in order to pinpoint those conditions that may need to be changed or improved. In these interviews the consultant often considers the following questions:

1. Why is this unit having the kinds of problems it has?
2. What keeps you personally from being as effective as you would like to be?
3. What things do you like best about this department or unit—things you want to continue?
4. What changes would make you and this unit more effective?
5. How could this unit begin to work more effectively together as a productive team?

Following the interviews, the consultant frequently does a content analysis of the interview, identifies the major themes or suggestions that emerge, and prepares a summary presentation. At the team-building meeting the consultant presents the summary, and the unit, under the manager's direction, analyzes the data and plans actions to deal with the major concerns.

Some consultants prefer not to conduct interviews prior to the team-building meeting and do not want to present a data summary. They have found that information shared in a private interview with a consultant is not as readily discussed in the open, with all other team members present, especially if some of those members have been the object of some of the interview information. Consultants have painfully discovered that people often deny their own interviews, fight the data, and refuse to use it as a basis of discussion and planning. At times it may be appropriate for the consultant to interview people privately to understand some of the deep-rooted issues but still have people present their own definitions of the problems in an open session. An alternative to interviewing is open data sharing.

*Open Sharing of Data.* In this method each person in the unit is asked to share data publicly with the other group members. The data shared may not be as inclusive as data revealed in an interview, but each person feels responsible to "own up" to the information he or she presents to the group and to deal with the issue raised. To prevent forced disclosure, one good ground rule is to tell people that they should raise only those issues they feel they can honestly discuss with the others. People will generally present only the information they feel comfortable discussing; thus the open sharing of data may result in less information but more willingness to "work the data."

The kinds of questions suggested for the interview format are the same ones that people share openly at the beginning of the team-building session. Each presents his or her views on what keeps the unit from being as effective as it could be or suggests reasons for a particular problem. Each person also describes the things he or she likes about the unit, those things that hinder personal effectiveness, and the changes he or she feels would be helpful. All of the data are compiled on a flip chart or chalkboard. (In another variation data for a large team could be gathered and shared in subgroups.) Then the group moves on to the next stage of the team-building cycle.

### Diagnosis and Evaluation of Data

With all of the data now available, the manager and the consultant must work with the group to summarize the data and put the information into a priority listing. The summary categories should be listed as one of the following:

A—issues that we can work on in this meeting

B—issues that someone else must work (and identify who the others would be)

C—issues that apparently are not open to change; that is, things we must learn to accept or live with

Category A items become the top agenda items for the rest of the team-building session. Category B items are those for which strategies must be developed for involving others. For category C items the group must plan coping mechanisms. If the manager is prepared, he or she can handle the summary and the category-development process. If the manager feels uneasy about this, the consultant may function as a role model to show how this is done.

The next important step is to review all of the data and to try to identify underlying factors that may be related to several problems. A careful analysis of the data may show that certain procedures, rules, or job assignments are causing several disruptive conditions.

### Problem Solving and Planning

After the agenda has been developed out of the data, the roles of the manager and the consultant diverge. The manager should move directly into the customary managerial role of group leader. The issues identified should become problems to solve, and plans for action should be developed.

While the manager is conducting the meeting, the consultant functions as a group observer and facilitator. Schein has referred to this activity as "process consulting,"[2] a function that others in the group can also learn to handle. In this role the consultant helps the group look at its problem-solving and work processes. He or she may stop the group if certain task or maintenance group functions are missing or being performed poorly. If the group gets bogged down or "steamrollered" into uncommitted decisions, the consultant helps look at these processes, why they occur, and how they can be avoided in the future. In this role the consultant is training the group to develop more group problem-solving and collaborative action-taking skills.

### Implementation and Evaluation

If the actions planned at the team-building session are to make any difference, they must be put into practice. Ensuring that

---

[2] E. H. Schein. *Op. cit.*, 1988.

plans are implemented has always been a major function of management. The manager must be committed to the team plans; without commitment, it is unlikely that a manager can be effective in holding people responsible for assignments agreed on in the team-building meeting.

The consultant's role is to observe the degree of action during the implementation phase and to be particularly active during the evaluation period. Another data-gathering process now begins, for that is the basis of evaluation. It is important to see if the actions planned or the goals developed during the team-building time have been achieved. This again should ultimately be the responsibility of the manager, but the consultant can be a help in training the manager to carry out good program evaluation.

The manager and the consultant should work closely together in any team-development effort. It is an ineffective program if the manager turns the whole effort over to the consultant with the plea, "You're the expert. Why don't you do it for me?" Such action leads to a great deal of dependence on the consultant, and, if the consultant is highly effective, it can cause the manager to feel inadequate or even more dependent. If the consultant is ineffective, the manager can then reject the plans developed as being unworkable or useless, and the failure of the team-building program is blamed on the consultant.

Managers should manage the enterprise. Consultants work with managers to help them plan and take action in unfamiliar areas where the manager may need to develop the skill and risk-taking attitude required to move into a new, potentially more profitable activity.

The consultant must be honest, aggressively forthright, and sensitive. He or she must be able to help the manager look at his or her own style and impact in either facilitating or hindering team effectiveness. The consultant needs to help group members get important data out in the open and keep them from feeling threatened for sharing with others. The consultant's role involves helping the group develop skills in group problem solving and planning. To do this the consultant must have a good feel for group processes and be willing to have the group look at its own dynamics. Finally, the consultant must feel a sense of pride and accomplishment when the manager and the team demonstrate their ability to solve problems independently and thus no longer need a consultant's services.

# 9

# Designing a Team-Building Program

The overall goal of any team-development program is to improve the effectiveness of a group that must work together to achieve results. According to Argyris, three conditions are characteristic of a healthy or effective organization or organizational unit: (1) the ability to gather relevant data; (2) the ability to make sound, free, and informed choices or decisions; and (3) the ability to implement those decisions with commitment.[1] In addition to these three conditions, most professionals working with teams would identify many of the factors listed in Chapter 2 as other characteristics of an effective team.[2] Given these characteristics, one goal of a team would be to maximize the development of such qualities into the team.

Another way of describing a team-building program is that its purpose is to help the work unit engage in a continual process of self-examination to gain awareness of those conditions that keep the unit from functioning effectively. Having gathered the data, the work group learns how to use the data for making decisions and then takes those actions that will lead to a growing state of health. Team development, in this sense, is a continual, ongoing process, not a one-time activity.

Team development often begins with a block of time, usually two or three days, during which the team starts learning

---

[1] C. Argyris, *Intervention Theory and Method* (Reading, Mass.: Addison-Wesley, 1970).

[2] J. R. Hackman, Ed., *Groups That Work (and Those That Don't): Creating Conditions for Effective Teamwork* (San Francisco: Jossey-Bass, 1989).

how to engage in its own review, analysis, action planning, decision making, and even action taking. Following the first meetings, the team may periodically take other blocks of time to continue the process, to review progress made since the last team meeting, and to identify what should be done to continue to improve the team's overall effectiveness. It is also possible that in time, the team will develop its skill for development to such a point that team members are continually aware of areas that need improvement and raise them at appropriate times with the appropriate people, thereby making it unnecessary to set aside a special meeting for such action.

There is no one way to put together a team-building program. The format will depend on the experience, interests, and needs of the team members; the experience and needs of the manager; the skills of the consultant (if one is needed); and the nature of the situation that has prompted the meeting. This chapter describes a range of design alternatives for each phase of a team-building program. Those planning such an activity may wish to select various design elements from among the alternatives that seem applicable to their own situation.

## Preparation

### Goals

The goals of this phase are to explain the purpose of team building, get commitment for participation, and do preliminary work for the team-building workshop. Any team-building program must be well conceived, and those involved must have indicated at least a minimal commitment to participate. Commitment will be increased if people understand clearly *why* the team-building program is being proposed and if they have an opportunity to influence the decision to go ahead with the program.

If this is the first time this group has spent some time together with the specific assignment to review their group effectiveness and to plan for change, participants will likely have a good deal of anxiety and apprehension. These concerns must be brought to the surface and handled.

Questions of deep concern probably will not be eliminated but may be reduced as a climate is set and as people "test the water" and find that plunging in is not all that difficult. Experience will be the best teacher and people will allay or confirm their fears as the session proceeds. Those conducting the session may anticipate such concerns and can raise them prior to the first meeting to reduce any extreme anxiety by openly describing what will happen and what the anticipated outcome will be.

### Alternative Actions

1. Have an outside person interview each unit member to identify problems, concerns, and need for change.
2. Invite an outside speaker to talk about the role of teams in organizations and the purposes of team development.
3. Gather data on the level of team effectiveness. (See Fig. 9.1 and the other instruments presented in this book.)
4. At a staff meeting have a general discussion about the need for a team-building program.
5. Invite a manager who has had a successful team-building experience to describe the activities and results in his or her unit.

## Start-Up

### Goals

The goals of this phase are to create a climate for work; to get people relaxed and loosened up; to establish norms for being open, for planning, and for dealing with issues; and to present a cognitive framework for the whole experience. The climate established during the start-up phase will, of course, influence the rest of the program.

### Alternative I

A. The superior can give a short opening talk, reviewing the goals as he or she sees them and the need for the program, emphasizing his or her support, and reaffirming the norm that no negative sanctions are intended for any open, honest behavior.
B. The role of the consultant, if there is one, can be explained by either the manager or the consultant.

**Figure 9.1**
*Team-Development Scale\**

**1. To what extent do I feel a real part of the team?**

| 1 | 2 | 3 | 4 | 5 |
|---|---|---|---|---|
| Completely a part all the time | A part most of the time | On the edge—sometimes in, sometimes out | Generally outside except for one or two short periods | On the outside, not really a part of the team |

**2. How safe is it in this team to be at ease, relaxed, and myself?**

| 1 | 2 | 3 | 4 | 5 |
|---|---|---|---|---|
| I feel perfectly safe to be myself; they won't hold mistakes against me. | I feel most people would accept me if I were completely myself, but there are some I am not sure about. | Generally one has to be careful what one says or does in this team. | I am quite fearful about being completely myself in this team. | I am not a fool; I would never be myself in this team. |

**3. To what extent do I feel "under wraps," that is, have private thoughts, unspoken reservations, or unexpressed feelings and opinions that I have not felt comfortable bringing out into the open?**

| 1 | 2 | 3 | 4 | 5 |
|---|---|---|---|---|
| Almost completely under wraps | Under wraps many times | Slightly more free and expressive than under wraps | Quite free and expressive much of the time | Almost completely free and expressive |

**4. How effective are we, in our team, in getting out and using the ideas, opinions, and information of all team members in making decisions?**

| 1 | 2 | 3 | 4 | 5 |
|---|---|---|---|---|
| We don't really encourage everyone to share their ideas, opinions, and information with the team in making decisions. | Only the ideas, opinions, and information of a few members are really known and used in making decisions. | Sometimes we hear the views of most members before making decisions, and sometimes we disregard most members. | A few are sometimes hesitant about sharing their opinions, but we generally have good participation in making decisions. | Everyone feels his or her ideas, opinions, and information are given a fair hearing before decisions are made. |

**5. To what extent are the goals the team is working toward understood, and to what extent do they have meaning for you?**

| 1 | 2 | 3 | 4 | 5 |
|---|---|---|---|---|
| I feel extremely good about goals of our team. | I feel fairly good, but some things are not too clear or meaningful. | A few things we are doing are clear and meaningful. | Much of the activity is not clear or meaningful to me. | I really do not understand or feel involved in the goals of the team. |

**6. How well does the team work at its tasks?**

| 1 | 2 | 3 | 4 | 5 |
|---|---|---|---|---|
| Coasts, loafs, makes no progress | Makes a little progress, but most members loaf | Progress is slow; spurts of effective work | Above average in progress and pace of work | Works well; achieves definite progress |

*(continued)*

**Figure 9.1**   *(continued)*

**7. Our planning and the way we operate as a team are largely influenced by:**

| 1 | 2 | 3 | 4 | 5 |
|---|---|---|---|---|
| One or two team members | A clique | Shifts from one person or clique to another | Shared by most of the members, but some are left out | Shared by all members of the team |

**8. What is the level of responsibility for work in our team?**

| 1 | 2 | 3 | 4 | 5 |
|---|---|---|---|---|
| Each person assumes personal responsibility for getting work done. | A majority of the members assume responsibility for getting work done. | About half assume responsibility; about half do not. | Only a few assume responsibility for getting work done. | Nobody (except perhaps one) really assumes responsibility for getting work done. |

**9. How are differences or conflicts handled in our team?**

| 1 | 2 | 3 | 4 | 5 |
|---|---|---|---|---|
| Differences or conflicts are denied, suppressed, or avoided at all costs. | Differences or conflicts are recognized but remain mostly unresolved. | Differences or conflicts are recognized, and some attempts are made to work them through by some members, often outside the team meetings. | Differences and conflicts are recognized, and some attempts are made to deal with them in our team. | Differences and conflicts are recognized, and the team usually is working them through satisfactorily. |

**10. How do people relate to the team leader, chairperson, or "boss"?**

| 1 | 2 | 3 | 4 | 5 |
|---|---|---|---|---|
| The leader dominates the team, and people are often fearful or passive | The leader tends to control the team, although people generally agree with the leader's direction. | There is some give and take between the leader and the team members. | Team members relate easily to the leader and usually are able to influence leader decisions. | Team members respect the leader, but they work together as a unified team, with everyone participating and no one dominant. |

*This scale was developed by William G. Dyer.

C. Participants may fill out and share their immediate here-and-now feelings about the meetings by responding to the following questions handed out on a sheet of paper. People call out their answers (to set the norm of open sharing of data), and the person at the flipchart records the responses:

**1.  How confident are you that any real change will result from these meetings?**

| 1 | 2 | 3 | 4 | 5 |
|---|---|---|---|---|
| Not confident at all | | Somewhat confident | | Highly confident |

**2.  To what degree do you feel that people really want to be here and work on team-development issues?**

| 1 | 2 | 3 | 4 | 5 |
|---|---|---|---|---|
| Don't really want to be here | | Some interest in being here | | High interest in being here |

**3.  How willing do you think people are to make changes that may be suggested?**

| 1 | 2 | 3 | 4 | 5 |
|---|---|---|---|---|
| Will be unwilling to change | | Some willingness to change | | Very willing to change |

**4.  How willing do you think you and others will be to express real feelings and concerns?**

| 1 | 2 | 3 | 4 | 5 |
|---|---|---|---|---|
| Not very willing | | Some degree of willingness | | Very willing |

The data can be tabulated, gathered, and presented to the group; for a group of eight people, the data might look as follows, with the profile line a connection of quickly estimated means:

| | 1 | 2 | | 3 | 4 | 5 |
|---|---|---|---|---|---|---|
| 1. | 1 ı | 2 ıı | X | 3 ıııı | 4 ı | 5 |
| 2. | 1 | 2 | | 3 ııı | 4 ııı | 5 ı |
| 3. | 1 | 2 ııı | X | 3 ıııı | 4 ı | 5 |
| 4. | 1 ı | 2 ıı | X | 3 ıııı | 4 ı | 5 |

The group of eight could then be divided into two groups of four and asked to discuss the questions, Why is this profile rather low? What would have to be done here to increase the positive orientation of people toward these meetings? Subgroups would then discuss for twenty minutes and report back to the total group.

The purpose of this type of beginning is to set the norm that the whole program is centered on data gathering, data analysis, open sharing, and trying to plan with data. This also allows group members to test the water about here-and-now data rather than more sensitive work-group issues, to see how people will respond and react to the questions.

### *Alternative II*

After preliminary remarks by the manager, the group members could be asked, In order for us to get a picture of how you see our group functioning, would each of you take a few minutes to describe our group as a kind of animal or combination of animals, a kind of machine, a kind of person, or whatever image comes to mind. Some groups in the past have been described as

- A hunting dog—a pointer. We run around and locate problems, then stop and point and hope that somebody else will take the action.

- A Cadillac with pedals. We look good on the outside, but there is no real power to get us moving.

- A Rube Goldberg device. Everything looks crazy and you can't imagine that anything will ever happen, but in some way, for some reason, we do get results at the end.

- An octopus. Each tentacle is out grasping anything it can but doesn't know what the other tentacles are doing.

As people share such images and explain what elicits the image, some questions may be asked: What are the common elements in these images? Do we like these images of ourselves? What do we need to do to change our image? Answering these questions becomes the major agenda item for subsequent group meetings.

### Alternative III

In this alternative the group is asked, usually by the consultant, to work on a major decision-making problem—such as the NASA exercise, Subarctic or Desert Survival,[3] Tinker Toy building, or the exercise Agree-Disagree Statements on Team Leadership, shown in Fig. 9.2—and to function under the direction of the superior in a fashion similar to the way they work on problems back home. The consultant acts as a process observer. After the exercise, the consultant has the group members review their own processes and determine both their strengths and their deficiencies in problem solving. The consultant shares his or her observations with the group. Lists of positive and negative features are compiled. The agenda for the following sessions is set, based on the question, How do we maximize our strengths and overcome deficiencies? For example, if the process review indicates that the group is very dependent on the leader, that some people are overwhelmed by the "big talker," and that the group jumps to decisions before everyone has a chance to put in ideas, the agenda is how to reduce or change these negative conditions.

## Group Problem Solving and Process Analysis

### Goals

In this phase one goal is to begin to take action on the problems identified. Assignments are made and dates are set for the completion of work. Another goal is for the team to practice better problem-solving, decision-making, planning, objective-selecting, and delegation skills.

Whatever the start-up method, or combination of methods used, this third phase usually involves two parts: (1) the work unit begins to engage in the problem-solving process; and (2) a process consultant or observer helps the group look at its skill in working on problems as an effective team, as a prelude to improving its problem-solving capabilities.

---

[3]See the exercises from Experimental Learning Methods, 39818 Plymouth Road, Plymouth, Mich. 48170.

**Figure 9.2**
*Agree-Disagree Statements on Team Leadership\**

**Instructions:** Read each statement once. Without conferring with anyone, indicate whether you agree (A) or disagree (D) with the statement. Then as a team discuss each statement and make a decision if you agree or disagree with the statement. Take sufficient time to understand each person's point of view. If your team cannot reach agreement, you may change the wording of the statement in order to reach agreement.

**Key:** "A" if you agree; "D" if you disagree.

( )  1. Effective team leaders consult with team members in order to collect information so they, the team leaders, can make a decision.

( )  2. Team leaders should involve team members in all decisions that affect them.

( )  3. Team leaders should take full responsibility for team decisions.

( )  4. Team leaders should not confront team members in front of other team members.

( )  5. A primary function of the team leader is to establish an atmosphere in which all team members feel free to express their feelings and opinions.

( )  6. The team leader should perceive and interact with team members as equals.

( )  7. The team leader should strive to help team members reach their potential even though that may result in one member's being "better" than another.

( )  8. A major responsibility of the team leader is to provide direction to the team and keep it on track.

( )  9. Maximum team effectiveness exists when there is a minimum amount of disagreement among team members.

( ) 10. The team leader is a "model" of effective team participation for other team members.

( ) 11. There are times when a team leader needs to use autocratic methods to get the team to function effectively.

*(continued)*

**Figure 9.2** *(continued)*

( ) 12. There are times when the team leader should ignore the feelings of a team member in order to reach a decision.

( ) 13. The team leader should exercise friendly but firm authority to effectively manage his or her team.

( ) 14. When the team leader is trying to do his or her best, team members should not be critical of those efforts.

( ) 15. There are times when the team leader should assign a task to an individual rather than the team just to save time.

---

*From Robert Dyer.

### Role of the Consultant

The process consultant or observer is usually trying to see to what extent the group is effective at both task activities and relationship-maintaining activities. Ineffective teams are often characterized by such conditions as:

- Domination by the leader
- Warring cliques or subgroups
- Unequal participation and uneven use of group resources
- Rigid or dysfunctional group norms and procedures
- A climate of defensiveness or fear
- Uncreative alternatives to problems
- Restricted communications
- Avoidance of differences or potential conflicts

Such conditions reduce the team's ability to work together in collective problem-solving situations. The role of the consultant is to help the group become aware of its processes and begin to develop greater group skills. Specifically, after becoming aware of a process problem, the group needs to establish a procedure, guideline, or plan of action to reduce the negative condition.

### Alternative I

Following the opening remarks, the consultant, outside person, or manager presents data that have been collected from the group members through interviews or instruments prior to the meeting. The group is asked to analyze the data: What do the data mean? Why do we respond the way we do? What conditions give rise to negative responses? What do we need to change to get a more positive response to our own organization?

This analysis can best be done in subgroups (three to four people) and then shared and compiled into a total listing of issues and possible change actions. The summaries form the basis for the subsequent sessions. The group also puts the data into categories, as described earlier. Category A items are the major work issues on the agenda.

### Alternative II

This design requires some extensive case analysis prior to the team-building sessions. An external consultant, a company OD person, or someone in management pulls together one or more studies, vignettes, or critical incidents that seem to represent some recurring problems in the work unit. Another possibility is to have each member write up a short case that represents a problem area for him or her. Again, the group task is to look at the several cases, try to discover what the underlying conditions are that trigger such conditions, and then plan action for reducing the likelihood that such conditions would occur again.

### Alternative III

In this method objective data gathered from records in the work unit are compiled and presented to the group members. Such information as the production records, grievance rate, absenteeism, turnover, lost time, budget discrepancies, late reports, cost increases, and so on are included in this feedback. The group's job is to conduct an in-depth analysis of the data, diagnose the course of negative trends, and then engage in action planning for improvement.

### Alternative IV

Instead of presenting data from prior data-collection methods to the group, data about the conditions or problems of the team are raised at the team meeting or in an agenda or problem or issues developed prior to the session. Each person is asked to come prepared to share his or her perception of the following: (1) What keeps this work group from functioning at its maximum potential? (2) What keeps you, personally, from doing the kind of job you would like to do? (3) What things do you like in this unit that you want to have maintained? (4) What changes would you like to see made that would help you and the whole group? Group members or the leader may have other items they would like to put on the agenda.

Each group member takes a turn sharing information. The responses are listed on newsprint, and common themes are identified. The most important issues are listed in priority, and they become the items for discussion.

### Problem-Solving Process

Regardless of the alternative selected, the work unit should, by this point, have identified a series of problems, concerns, or issues. The team next must move into a problem-solving process by engaging in the following actions:

1. Put problems in order of priority and select the five or six most pressing problems to be addressed during the workshop.

2. Begin the classic problem-solving process: Define the problem, list alternative solutions, select alternative to be implemented, develop an action plan, perform the action, and evaluate the results.

3. Work out forcefield analysis.[4] Identify the existing level of group effectiveness, formulate a goal, identify driving and restraining forces, and develop a plan to remove restraining forces.

4. Begin role negotiations. Negotiate between people or subunits the actions needed from each other to improve effectiveness.

---

[4]Kurt Lewin, "Group Discussion and Social Change," in Maccoby et al., Eds., *Readings in Social Psychology* (New York: Holt, 1958) and W. G. Dyer, *Strategies for Managing Change* (Reading, Mass.: Addison-Wesley, 1984), Chapter 2.

5. Set up task-force teams or subunits. Give each team a problem to work on. Set up the actions, carry out the action, and assess the results.

6. After all problems have been listed, the group sorts them into categories based on those problems (a) we can work on here; (b) someone else must handle (and identify who that is); (c) we must live with, since they appear to be beyond our ability to change.

7. Set targets, objectives, or goals. The group spends time identifying short- or long-range goals it wishes to achieve, makes assignments, and sets target dates for completion.

## Interpersonal, Subunit, and Group Feedback

Often a major issue following the identification of problems is the sharing of feedback to individuals, subparts of the team, or the work group as a whole. Certain actions, functions or personal styles, and strategies on the part of one or more people may be hindering the teamwork and preventing achievement of goals and satisfaction for certain other team members. If such is the case it may be legitimate to engage in an open feedback session.

### *Goals*

This phase is designed to share feedback among people in such a way as to help them improve their effectiveness and to give feedback to work units with the same objective in mind. The goal of a feedback session is to share data about performance so that difficulties can be resolved. It is critical that a feedback session *not* slip into name calling, personal griping, or verbal punishing of others. All feedback given should reflect a genuine willingness to work cooperatively: "My performance suffers because of some things that happen in which you are involved. Let me share my feelings and reactions so you can see what is happening to me. I would like to work out a way that we all can work more productively together."

### *Types of Feedback*

Feedback is most helpful if it can be given in descriptive fashion or in the form of suggestions.

***Descriptive Feedback.***  "John, when you promise me that you will have a report ready at a certain time (as happened last Thursday) and I don't get it, that really frustrates me. It puts me behind schedule and makes me feel very resentful toward you. Are you aware that such things are going on, and how should we work out this kind of problem?"

***Suggestions.***  "John, let me make a suggestion that would really be of help to me as we work together. If you could get your reports to me on time, particularly those that have been promised at a certain time, it would help my work schedule and reduce my frustration. Also, if I don't get a report on time, what would you prefer I do about it?"

***Other Possibilities.***  Following are some other ways group members go about sharing feedback with one another:

1. Each person has a sheet of newsprint on the wall. Each team member writes on the sheets of other members items in three areas: (a) things that person should *begin* doing that will increase his or her effectiveness; (b) things the individual should *stop* doing; and (c) things he or she should *continue* to do.

2. Envelope exchange. Each person writes a note to others, covering the same issues as in item 1, and gives the notes to the other team members.

3. Confirmation-disconfirmation process. Group members summarize how they view themselves and their own work performance—their strengths and areas that need improvement. Others are asked to confirm or disconfirm the person's diagnosis.

4. Management profile. Each person presents the profile of his or her effectiveness from previously gathered data (from instruments like the BSR Management Profile, Telometrics Profile, and Scientific Methods Grid Profile). The group confirms or disconfirms the profile.

5. Analysis of subunits. If the team has subunits, each subunit is discussed in terms of what it does well, what it needs to change, and what it needs to improve.

6. Total unit or organizational analysis.[5] The group looks at how it has been functioning and critiques its own performance over the past year, identifying things it has done well and areas that need improvement.

7. Open feedback session. Each person who would like feedback may ask for it in order to identify areas of personal effectiveness and areas that need improvement.

8. Prescription writing. Each person writes a prescription for others: "Here is what I would prescribe that you do (or stop doing) in order to be more effective in your position." Prescriptions are then exchanged.

## Action Planning

The end result of all the activities mentioned so far is to help the work unit identify those conditions that are blocking both individual and group effectiveness, so that the group can begin to develop plans for action and change. Decisions for action should be made with a commitment to carry such action to completion.

### Goals

The goal of this phase is to confirm and pinpoint changes, goals, assignments, and dates for completion. During this phase, plans are developed, assignments are given, procedures are outlined, and dates are set for completion and review. Often the plan is a set of agreements on who is willing to take a specific action. All such agreements should be written down, circulated, and followed up later to ensure that they have been carried out.

### Options for Action Planning

Following is a set of actions that are possible during this phase:

1. Each person takes time to evaluate his or her feedback and develops a plan of action for personal improvement. This plan is presented to the others.

2. Contract negotiations.[6] If there are particular problems between individuals or subunits, specific agreements

---

[5]R. W. Boss, *Organization Development in Health Care* (Reading, Mass.: Addison-Wesley, 1989), Part II.

[6]R. Harrison, "Role Negotiations: A Tough-Minded Approach to Team Development," in W. Burke and H. Hornstein, Eds., *The Social Technology of Organization Development* (Washington, D.C.: NTL Learning Resources, 1971).

for dealing with conflict issues are drawn up and signed.

3. Assignment summary. Each person summarizes what his or her assignments are and the actions he or she intends to take as a follow-up of the team-development meeting.

4. Subunit or group plans. If development plans have been completed, they are presented and reviewed.

5. Schedule review. The group looks at its time schedule and its action plans. Dates for completion and dates for giving progress reports on work being done are confirmed. The next staff meeting is scheduled. If another team-development workshop or meeting is needed, it may be scheduled at this time.

## Follow-Up

Unless the decisions made and actions planned are implemented, the functioning team will not improve. Therefore it is important to schedule follow-up meetings and to review decisions and actions. The manager in charge must manage the follow-up efforts. If a good three-day team-building meeting is held but the resulting excitement and enthusiasm are allowed to dissipate because of a lack of follow-through, the level of effectiveness of the work unit may decrease, and the team-building meetings will have had, in the long run, a negative effect.

### Goals

The major goals in this phase are to establish a system that will ensure that actions agreed on and agreements made are, in fact, implemented. Clear deadlines are set, and the regular processes of management are followed to ensure completion. A major goal is to see that continual team building becomes a part of the ongoing activities of the work group.

### Courses of Action

In the follow-up phase certain alternative courses of action are possible. A more extensive discussion of the follow-up process is presented in Chapter 12.

1. Process review. At the end of the workshop, time may be taken to critique the team-development program— things that went well, things that need to be changed, recommendations for the next team-development meeting, and so on.

2. Management review and follow-through. All assignments and action plans are reviewed by appropriate managers or management groups to make sure that the plans are supported and reviewed and that commitments called for at appropriate dates have been set.

3. Task forces or committees may have been formed. Specific dates are set to have these work groups report on the results of their efforts.

4. Following the initial team-building meeting, shorter periods of time may be used to have a continuation of the first team-building meeting. It may be possible to have a four-hour block to review the work done since the last meeting, gather new data, make new assignments, and plan for the next session. Team building in this manner becomes an ongoing process.

# 10

## Handling Conflict and Confusion in Teams

### The Team in Conflict

Sometimes the basic problem in a work unit is the prevalence of highly disruptive conflict and hostility. Feelings of animosity between individuals or between cliques or subgroups may have grown to such proportions that people who must work together do not speak to one another at all. Communications are all by memo, even though offices are adjoining. Why do such conflicts occur, and how can a work group resolve such differences?

Probably the most common "explanation" for understanding conflict is the theory of conflicting personalities. When two people do not get along, a commonplace explanation is to say that their "personalities" clash. Underlying this is a presumption that one individual's personality (a complex of attitudes, values, feelings, needs, and experiences) is so different from another's that the two just cannot function compatibly. Since one's personality is so deeply rooted by the adult stage of life, it seems almost impossible to improve the situation.

### *Expectation Theory of Conflict*

A more useful way to understand conflict is to view it as the result of a violation of expectations. Whenever the behavior of one person violates the expectations of another, negative reactions will result. If agreement is not reached, the continued cycle of violated expectations and the application of negative sanctions can escalate until open expressions of hostility are common, and the two people are trying to hurt or punish each other in various ways rather than trying to work cooperatively. People's expectations of others can be described in terms of *what* is to be done, *when* it should be done, and *how* it is to be done. Frequently people may agree on the *what* conditions, but the violations occur in the other two aspects, namely, when actions should be taken or how they should be fulfilled.

One R&D department in a large corporation was split by conflict, with two warring factions of professionals. One group of development researchers felt that the other group got more favors, better facilities, and more rewards. This group's expectations were continually being violated. Members of this group expected more sharing of research results, more common decision making, more meetings, and more equal distribution of rewards. When these expectations were not met, the group reacted negatively. These negative responses in turn violated the expectations of the other faction, whose members reciprocated with their own critical reactions. Before long the department was filled with unpleasant feelings of hostility.

Expectation theory allows for a greater possibility for dealing with conflict, for it focuses on *behavior*. If the one faction in the R&D department can begin to identify the behaviors or actions that violate its expectations, perhaps agreements can be negotiated, so that the end result is people rewarding one another rather than applying punishments.

### Negotiating Agreements

In planning a team-building session to deal with conflicts, certain agreements between the clashing parties need to be met.

1. All parties must agree to come together and work on the problems

2. It helps if people can agree that problems exist, that those problems should be solved, and that all parties have some responsibility to work on the issues.

3. People may find it easier to deal with conflict if they can accept the position that the end result of the team-building session is not to get everyone to "like" one another but rather to understand one another and to be able to work together. People do not need to form personal friendships, but group members should be able to at least trust one another and meet one another's expectations.

In setting up the team-building session, the disagreeing parties will work best together if they can adopt the position that it is not productive to try and unravel who is at fault or what "caused" the problems. Rather, they should accept the fact that differences exist and that they need to work out agreeable solutions.

***The Start-Stop-Continue Format.*** When parties come together in the team-building session, each party builds a list for the other. Each lists the things it would like to see the other individual or group start doing, stop doing, and continue to do if its expectations are to be met and positive results achieved. The parties then share their lists. If there is general conflict in the team—not between parties—each person lists what the total team needs to start doing, stop doing, or continue doing to reduce conflicts and disruptions.

***Negotiation.*** With the lists of things that each party wants from the other on display for all to see, a negotiation session ensues. Subgroup or person A identifies what it wants from subgroups or person B and vice versa. The two units then agree on what one party will do in return for an equal behavioral alteration on the part of the other. Such agreements can be written up. In some cases signing the agreement increases the commitment to making the change. Such a process puts the formerly warring factions into a problem-solving situation that requires them to try to work out solutions rather than spending their time finding fault, placing blame, or looking for causes of the problems. This negotiation process has been the basis for a companywide team-development program in the Diamond Shamrock Company.[1]

The design of such a conflict-reducing meeting can vary widely. It may be desirable to precede the session with a presentation of expectation theory and to describe the negative consequences of continued hostility. Another possibility is to have members of each party try to predict what the other party thinks about them and what they think the other wants from them. These guesses are often surprisingly accurate and may facilitate the coming to agreement.

---

[1] Arthur M. Louis, "They're Striking Some Strange Bargains at Diamond Shamrock," *Fortune*, January 1976:142–157.

This design may also be used to negotiate agreements between individuals. If a manager feels that the thing most divisive in the team is conflict between two people, the two may be brought together for a problem-solving situation in order to begin to work out agreements with each other. If there are disagreements in the team at any point, it is often well to stop and work out a negotiation and come to an agreement.

Negotiation is often a compromise situation. Each party gives up something to receive something of similar value from the other. Too frequently, however, conflicts are handled by people engaging in

1. *Ignoring*—trying to pretend that no disagreement exists.

2. *Smoothing*—trying to placate people and attempting to get them to feel good even though an agreement has not been reached.

3. *Forcing*—getting agreement from a position of power. If the more powerful person forces the other to agree, the result may be public agreement but private resistance.

When conflict occurs in an effective team, time is taken to identify the cause of the conflict. The conflict is identified as a problem to be solved, and problem-solving actions are taken.[2]

## The Team in Confusion

Sometimes a group has worked together for years, but either basic assignments were never clarified or conditions have changed and old role definitions are no longer adequate. Following is a description of a team-building model designed to reduce problems arising out of unclear assignments or relationships. Most teams have never spent adequate time making sure that all members understand their roles and what is expected of them. When confusion is the diagnosis, the following model is very useful.

---

[2]For more on dealing with conflict, see R. E. Walton, *Managing Conflict: Interpersonal Dialogue and Third-Party Roles, Second Edition* (Reading, Mass.: Addison-Wesley, 1987).

### *The Role-Clarification Model*

The role-clarification model of team building is considered appropriate if several of the following conditions are prevalent in the organization or unit considering a team-building program.

1. The unit is newly organized and people are not clear as to what others do and what others expect of them.

2. Changes and reassignments have been made in the unit and there is a lack of clarity as to how the various functions and positions now fit together under the new arrangements.

3. Job descriptions are old. Staff meetings are held infrequently and then only for passing on needed directions. People carry out their assignments with very little contact with others in the same office. People generally feel isolated.

4. Conflicts and interpersonal disruptions in the unit seem to be increasing. Coffee-break talk and other information communications center on discussion of overlaps and encroachments on work assignments from others. People get requests they don't understand. People hear about what others are doing through the grapevine; it sounds like something they should know about but nobody gets them together.

5. The boss engages primarily in one-to-one management. Staff meetings are infrequent or are held primarily for hearing the boss raise issues with one individual at a time while others watch and wait for their turn. Almost no problem solving is done as a total staff or between people. Issues are taken to the boss, and only then are needed people called together.

6. People sit in their offices and wonder, "What is happening in this outfit? I don't know what others are doing, and I'm sure nobody knows (or cares) what I'm doing."

7. A crisis occurs because everyone thought someone else was responsible for handling a situation that was never covered.

### Planning

**Time Commitment.**   For a staff of eight to ten people, the minimum time needed for this type of design is approximately one hour for each person, or a total of eight to ten hours of meeting time, preferably in a solid block. With a training day from 8:30 to 12:00 and 1:00 to 4:30, this could be achieved in one and a half training days. It would also be possible to conduct this type of team-building session by taking out one afternoon a week over a period of time, such as three afternoons in one week or one afternoon for three weeks. Our experience, however, indicates that the time spent in one block allows for more impact to occur. Each time a group meets, a certain amount of "settling-in" time occurs, which is minimized if the sessions are held at one time.

**Resource Personnel.**   If the ground rules, procedures, overall goals, and design elements are clear, a manager need not be afraid to conduct this type of meeting with no outside assistance from a consultant or facilitator. If certain realistic concerns suggest that an outside person would be helpful in facilitating the meeting, one could be included. This person may be someone from within the company but in a different department (such as an OD specialist) or a consultant from outside the company.

Regardless of whether an outside resource person is used, the entire team-building meeting should be conducted and "managed" by the senior administrator or boss. Team building is management's business; it is a supervisor building his or her team. It is *not* an exercise called by a staff person in personnel.

### Program Design

**Goal.** The goal of a role-relationship team-building program is to arrive at that condition where all members of a work unit can publicly agree that they

- Have a clear understanding of the major requirements of their own job
- Feel that the others at the team-building meeting also clearly understand everyone's position and duties
- Know what others expect of them in their working relationships
- Feel that all know what others need from them in their working relationships

All agreements in working relationships are reached with a spirit of collaboration and a willingness to implement the understandings. Procedures are established that permit future misunderstandings to be handled in a more effective way.

*Preparation.* This part of the team-building activity can be done prior to the session or should be done first by each member of the group in private as the team session begins. Each person should prepare answers to the following questions:

1. What do you feel the organization expects you do to in your job? (This may include the formal job description.)
2. What do you do in your job? (The working activities are described, and any discrepancies between the formal job description and the person's job activities are pointed out.)
3. What do you need to know about other people's jobs that would help you do your work?
4. What do you feel others should know about your job that would help them do their work?
5. What do you need from others in order to do your job the way you would like?
6. What do others need from you that would help them do their work?

### Meeting Design

All meetings of the team-building program should be conducted by the unit manager. If a consultant is present, he or she should be a resource but should not conduct the sessions.

*Goals.* The goals of the team-building meeting should be presented, clarified, and discussed. Everyone should agree on the goals or hoped-for outcomes of the sessions.

*Ground Rules.* Ground rules for each function should be developed from the group, written on a sheet of paper, and posted for all to see. Some suggested ground rules are as follow:

1. Each person should be as candid and open as possible in a spirit of wanting to help improve the team.

2. A person who wants to know how another person feels or thinks on an issue should ask that person directly. The person asked should give an honest response, even if it is to say, "I don't feel like responding right now."

3. If the meeting becomes unproductive for any person, he or she should express this concern to the group.

4. Each person should have an opportunity to speak on every issue.

5. Decisions made should be agreeable to all persons affected by the decision.

### Role Clarification

Each person will be the focal person and will follow these steps:

1. The focal person describes his or her job as he or she sees it. This means sharing all information about how the focal person understands the job—*what* is expected, *when* things are expected to be done, and *how* they are expected to be done. Other team members have the right to ask questions for clarification.

2. After the focal person describes his or her understanding of the requirements of the positions, all others are to show that they understand what that person's position entails: what is to be done, when things are to be done, and how they are to be done.

3. If the focal person and others have differences in expectations, they should be resolved at this point, so that there is a common agreement about what the focal person's job entails.

4. After agreement has been reached about the nature of the job, the focal person talks directly to each person, identifying what he or she needs from the other in order to do the job as agreed on.

5. The others then tell the focal person what they may need in return if they are to work together so that the focal person can accomplish the demands of the position.

### Conclusion

At the end of the sessions, the entire team-building program should be critiqued. People should respond to the following questions:

1. How have you felt about the team-building meetings?
2. What were the best parts for you?
3. What needed to be changed or improved?
4. Do we need other sessions like this? If so, what should we discuss? When should we meet again?

This type of team-development meeting is one of the easiest to manage and one of the most productive of all design possibilities for improving team effectiveness. Most groups of people slip into areas of ambiguity in their working relationships. Expectations about performances get formed that people do not understand or even know about. The periodic clarification of roles is a useful process for any working group.

One company's executive committee was conducting a role-clarification meeting. The members of the president's management group were outlining their jobs as they saw them and identifying what they felt they needed from one another in order to carry out their jobs more effectively. When her turn came, the personnel manager turned to the president and said, "One of the actions I need from you is a chance to get together with you a couple of times a year and review my performance and see what things you feel I need to do to improve."

The president asked in surprise, "Why do you need to get together with me?"

Responded the personnel manager, "When I was hired two years ago, it was my understanding that I was to report directly to you."

"Nobody ever cleared that with me," stated the president. "I thought you reported to the executive vice-president."

The personnel manager had been waiting for two years for a chance to get directions and instructions from the person she thought was her direct superior, but that relationship had never been clarified until the role-clarification session.

## The Boss as the Center of Conflict

It is a rather common occurrence to find that the center of conflict is the superior or team leader. Sometimes the problem is between the boss and the total group and sometimes between the boss and one or two members. Either way, unless the superior is aware of the situation and is willing to take steps to remedy the problem, it is difficult for members to open up the issue and deal with it. It is also not uncommon for the superior to be totally or partially unaware of the extent of the emotional breach that has occurred. In power relationships subordinates have learned to become quite skilled at masking negative feelings and pretending everything is going well when in fact there is "trouble in River City." Sometimes feelings are not completely masked and instead a form of passive-aggressive resistance occurs that the superior may see but not understand.

It would seem realistic that when any of the major symptoms of team difficulties (as listed in Chapter 8) emerge, the team leader should wonder, "Is it possible that I am at least partly responsible for these problems?" How does a team leader get a decent answer to this question?

1. *Ask the team members.* Either in a team meeting or in an interview one-on-one with the team members, the team leader might say something like this: "I want you to level with me. I know that things have not been going well in our unit (describe some of the symptoms). I want to know if I am responsible for creating negative reactions in the group. I would appreciate it if you could let me know either openly now or in a memo later what things I am doing that create problems and any suggestions you have that would improve matters."

   In asking for feedback, it is often useful if the leader can identify some things that have already come to mind—essentially priming the feedback pump. For example, "I think that I sometimes come to meetings with my mind already made up and then put pressures on people to agree with me; then when I get the forced agreement, I pretend that we have reached a consensus. Do you see this behavior in me? (Wait for a response.) If you do, what suggestions do you have that will help me avoid this kind of problem?"

   If there is a lack of trust in the group or in certain team members, this direct asking may not elicit any real data or at best only hidden messages. This means that the leader may then need to resort to other means of getting data.

2. *Use an outside resource.* A common method of getting information to the leader is to find an outside person, either outside the team but in the organization (an HR specialist) or an external consultant. A skilled outside resource can interview team members and try to elicit data about the involvement of the team leader in team problems. This information can then be fed back to the leader and a strategy devised for using the information with the team.

3. *Use instruments.* Currently a wide variety of instruments is available for gathering data, anonymously if necessary, from subordinates about their perceptions of the leader. These data need to be gathered and analyzed by someone other than the boss to ensure anonymity. An HR person is useful for handling this task and then seeing that the data are summarized and returned to the superior. Then a method for using this information with the team needs to be devised. A recommended method is for the manager to present a summary of data to the group, indicate acceptance of the data, announce some preliminary actions that will be taken, and ask the team members to suggest other appropriate changes.

4. *Undertake laboratory training.* A method used more often some years back than today is for the manager to go to a training program that features giving feedback to all participants on their interpersonal style. The manager then brings a summary of this feedback to the team, checks with them about its validity, and works out a program of improvement. Such laboratory programs are still conducted by the National Training Laboratories, UCLA Business School Extension, Behavioral Science Resource, and others.

Although the superior wishing to find out if his or her performance is causing conflicts in the team may take a variety of actions, a more difficult issue remains if the leader is unaware of his or her impact or does not seem to want to find out. In such a situation how do team members get data to the leader?

1. *Suggest a role-clarification session.* Such a session could allow the team members to identify actions they need from the team leader or changes they feel would improve activities in the team.

2. *Give direct feedback.* Obviously one possibility is for team members to find an opportunity to give direct, albeit unsolicited, feedback to the leader. Despite the inherent risks, the team—either altogether or through representatives—could say to the leader, "We have a dilemma. There are problems in the team that we feel involve you. Our dilemma is, we think we should share this information with you, but we do not want to disrupt our relationship with you. Do you have any suggestions as to how we might deal with this dilemma?" This approach usually results in the leader's asking for the data in a far different atmosphere than confronting the leader unexpectedly with tough feedback.

3. *Use an outside person.* It is also possible for the team to go to an appropriate internal resource person (an HR person) and ask for assistance. Often the outside person can then go to the leader and suggest a set of alternative actions that might surface the concerns for some kind of action taking.

## The Problem Member

One of the most commonly asked questions is, What do you do when one member of the team continually blocks the rest of the unit? This person may always take a contrary point of view, vote against proposals everyone else supports, take a negative or pessimistic position on everything, and frequently miss meetings or not follow through on assignments.

The obvious question in response is, Why do you keep a person like that in your organization? Usually the answer is that this person has some needed competencies, is a long-time employee, and terminating or transferring someone has a lot of built-in problems. However, if a manager or supervisor is trying to build a team and one person won't buy into the process, some method of eliminating that person should be considered.

The following kinds of action have also been found to be successful in some (not all) cases.

1. *Direct confrontation between the team leader and the problem person.* This may give the supervisor an opportunity to describe clearly the problem behaviors and the consequences if such behaviors do not change.

2. *Confrontation by the group.* If only the boss deals with the problem person, the conflict may be perceived by that person as just the personal bias of the boss. In a case like this, it would be better for the group to deal directly with the problem member collectively in a team meeting. The team members must be descriptive, not evaluative. They must describe the problem behavior and identify the negative consequences of the behaviors—all without punitive, negative evaluations of the individual personally.

3. *Special responsibility.* It has been found for some difficult people, giving them a more controlling role in the team increases their commitment to the team process. The person might be asked to be the team recorder, the agenda builder, or the one to summarize the discussion of issues. One team even rotated the difficult member into the role of *acting* team leader with the responsibility for a limited time of getting team agreement on the issues at hand.

4. *Limited participation.* One team asked the problem person to attend meetings, listen but not participate in the team activities, and then have a one-to-one session with the team leader. If the leader felt that the member had some legitimate issues to raise, the leader would present them to the group at the next meeting, but in all cases the discussion of the team would be final.

5. *External assignment.* At times it may be possible to give the problem person an assignment outside the activities of the rest of the team. The person may make a contribution to the work unit on an individual basis, whereas the bulk of the work that requires collaboration is handled by the rest of the team.

All of these suggestions are useful when the person is a serious obstruction to the working of the group. One must always be careful, however, to differentiate the real problem person from someone who sees things differently and whose different view or perspectives need to be listened to and considered with the possibility that this may enrich the productivity of the team. Teams can get *too* cohesive and isolate a person who is different.

# 11

# Developing the Temporary Team

The use of temporary groups or teams, variously called committees, task forces, work groups, or project teams, is widely practiced in most organizations. This collection of people must come together and in a relatively short time (usually from six weeks to a year) come up with recommendations, make decisions, or take specific actions that are carefully thought through and useful. To accomplish these goals in a relatively short time with people who already have full-time assignments elsewhere in the organization, the team must come together and quickly coalesce and be productive almost immediately.

## Preliminary Conditions for Temporary Teams

Temporary teams are usually constrained by time. They are generally of short duration and have limited time for any given session. Therefore members often feel under pressure to dive immediately into the work at hand and are reluctant to spend the equivalent of a total day to get acquainted, understand the goals, plan how the group will work, make realistic assignments, and build some commitment to one another—in other words, becoming a real team.

An old case study of two groups, each appointed to function for about a year, highlights the importance of team formation to the group's later functioning. One group was a high school science curriculum committee asked to try and coordinate a unified curriculum for all the science classes in the high school. The other was the Atomic Energy Committee under the direction of

David Lillienthal, which was given the charge to develop the guidelines for the control and use of atomic energy in the United States following the blasts over Hiroshima and Nagasaki in World War II. It is reported that at the end of the year, the high school group had nothing to show for its efforts and declared the problem too complex to solve by a committee. The Atomic Energy Committee completed an extensive document that outlined the policies for the use of atomic energy for the nation, and this report became the basis of national policy in this area.

The case analysis showed that a major difference between the two groups was the way they began. The curriculum group plunged immediately into work and struggled for a year because it could not deal with different ideas, opinions, and recommendations and found itself riddled with conflict almost from the beginning. The Atomic Energy group started differently. During the first several meetings, members spent time getting acquainted with one another and developing some guidelines for working. This group adopted as one of its important operating principles the notion that all members were intelligent, committed, productive people. Therefore if any group member said that he or she did not understand something, did not agree with something, or felt lost or confused, all members said, "We are therefore all confused or not in agreement or not fully understanding, and we must review everything again." The group did not want to have subgroups forming because of different ideas; nor did the group want members to belittle someone by saying, in essence, "Why are you so stupid you can't understand? You are holding us up. Get on board and agree so we can move ahead." In other words, in order to achieve the goal of becoming a productive temporary team, team members need to agree that they will spend enough time preparing to work before they start into work.

Another important preliminary condition is to give the temporary team adequate authority to get the work done. A few years ago, a major U.S. automobile company found itself behind its competitors in important design features. An analysis showed that temporary design teams made up of people from several basic functional departments (engineering, R&D, production, etc.) took as much as a year longer than competitors to come up with new designs. Further analysis also disclosed that most team members were told by their superiors in their functional departments, "Don't you make any final decisions until you come back and check with me." This meant that decisions in the design team were continually being postponed while team members checked back with functional bosses. These delays were not stopped until the design teams were given authority to make key decisions without checking back with departments.

The major tasks facing the temporary team are basically the same as for one that has worked together. Team members must build a relationship, establish a facilitative emotional climate, and work out methods for: (1) setting goals, (2) solving problems, (3) making decisions, (4) ensuring follow-through and completion of tasks, (5) developing collaboration of effort, (6) establishing open lines of communication, and (7) ensuring an appropriate support system that will let people feel accepted and yet keep issues open for discussion and disagreement. One advantage the temporary team has over an established unit in a team-building situation is that is does not have to break down any barriers, bad habits, useless or harmful stereotypes or attitudes, inappropriate working relations, or procedures that have been formed and are sometimes set rigidly in the concrete of human habit. Generally the new team can start its activities by asking, How can we set in motion the kinds of actions that will allow us to work together and get our goals accomplished and leave us feeling good about ourselves and one another?

## Design for a New Temporary Team

When a temporary team is being formed, members must first meet long enough for people to get acquainted and to set guidelines and procedures for work. The design of a new temporary team consists of several distinct steps.

### Step 1. Developing a Realistic Priority Level

Often people who are put together on a new team, frequently by assignment, have slightly differing levels of priority or commitment to the work of the team. Some may see it as a highly significant assignment and worthy of a great deal of time and energy. Others may see it as important but lower on their personal priority list, and yet others may see it as low in both importance and priority. To come to grips with the priority issue, team members can do the following:

1. Using the scale shown in Fig. 11.1, have each person draw a vertical line that represents his or her total work requirements and their priorities. Each person marks the point that represents where this team assignment ranks as a priority activity (see Fig. 11.1).

2. Next, have each person write down the amount of time he or she is willing to commit to the work of the team over a month's time.

3. Summarize the priority rankings (see Fig. 11.1) and also the time commitments. Note the range of times and priorities and also the averages for the two dimensions.

4. In the group let each person who desires explain his or her priority and time rankings and then come to agreement as to a realistic amount of time and energy that can be expected of the team as a whole. Persons with a higher priority and team commitments may be allowed to accept heavier assignments. Making this decision

**Figure 11.1**
*Priority and Time Rankings*

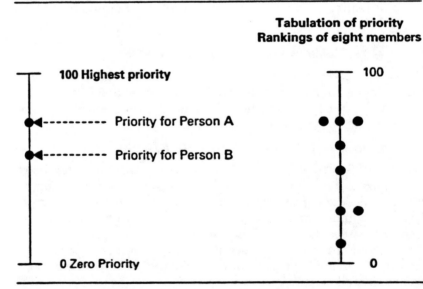

openly reduces the resentment some have for doing more work and guilt of others for letting them.

Understanding the priority of time and commitment is especially important for a temporary team. This step may not be useful for a new team that will continue to stay together.

### Step 2. Sharing Expectations

Give five minutes for each person to think about and get ready to respond to the following questions:

- What worries you most or is your biggest concern about working on this team?
- How would this team function if everything went just as you hoped?
- What would this team be like if everything went wrong?
- What actions do you think must be taken to ensure the positive outcomes?

Each person has an opportunity to share reactions; everyone responds to each question in turn. Try to identify the major concerns people have and list them on a blackboard or newsprint. These concerns should become items on a planning agenda as conditions to take into consideration in order to ensure that positive things are achieved.

### Step 3. Clarifying Goals

Having established priority and commitment levels and identified positive and negative expectations, the new team is ready to clarify its goals and objective. The team should discuss and then write down what members agree is the group's *core mission*—a statement of the basic function or "reason for being" for that group, committee, or team. All plans and actions should be evaluated against the core mission. The question to continually ask is, If we continue the activities already outlined, will we accomplish our core mission? Extending from the core mission are the subgoals and specific objectives for a given period of time.

For example, the Edgemont Company formed a task force to review all training and development activities in the company and to make some recommendations for a coordinated training and development effort. The task force met and established its core mission: The mission of this task force is to ensure an appropriate and effective thrust in management and organization development in the Edgemont Company.

Subgoals were then identified. The team agreed to try to accomplish the core mission by: (1) reviewing all ongoing training and development programs; (2) assessing the effectiveness of these programs; (3) determining if there are any overlaps or major gaps in training and development; (4) constructing a model of an effective program; (5) making recommendations to the executive committee as to the type of program needed; (6) assisting, if needed, in the implementation of the recommendations; and (7) assisting in evaluating the consequences or results of the implemented recommendations.

Once the core mission and specified subgoals have been set, the task force can make specific assignments to its members.

### Step 4. Formulating Operating Guidelines

The new team needs to establish guidelines for how it will work. Provisions also need to be formulated for changing the guidelines if they prove to be dysfunctional or inappropriate as conditions change. The guidelines should clarify actions and roles and should reduce the ambiguity or mixed expectations of people as to how things ought to function, which is the basis of a great deal of conflict in a working group. Following are some of the areas for which guidelines may be useful.

**How Will We Make Decisions?**   It is useful for the new team to talk about its decision-making procedures. Do members want to make all decisions by majority vote or team consensus, or do they want to leave some decisions to subgroups that are assigned to work?

If the group opts to make decisions by consensus, all should realize that this does not mean unanimity (everyone thinking alike). A consensus is a decision hammered out by permitting everyone to have a say. Consensus is reached after discussion, give-and-take, and compromise—when people can honestly say, "This is a sound decision—one that I am willing *to support and implement*. It is not exactly what I personally want, but given the range of opinions, the time factor, and the kinds of personalities involved, it is a good working decision."

Unless *everyone* can take that position, a consensus has not been reached. Discussion would need to continue, and adjustments or compromises or new alternatives would have to be explored until a solution is found that results in team consensus.

***What Will Be Our Basic Method for Work?*** The team should decide what it feels will be the most efficient way to get work done. Should the total group consider all items? Should people do individual work that is then submitted to the group? Or should subcommittees do the initial work? All of these methods may be used, depending on the nature of the work to be done. However, the method of work should be decided at the outset.

***How Do We Make Sure that Everyone Gets a Chance to Discuss Issues or Raise Concerns?*** If a team is to be effective, members need to feel that they can discuss and have considered issues or concerns they deem important. How will the team ensure this condition? It may be agreed that any members can put any item of concern on the agenda for the next meeting. An "open" meeting might be scheduled periodically to allow discussion of any topic or issue. Time could be reserved at the end of certain meetings for an open discussion. Members could be asked to distribute a memo identifying the issue they want discussed.

***How Will We Resolve Differences?*** Any working group will have times when individuals or subgroups disagree. If not handled or managed, disagreements can, at the least, waste time and may even split the group into warring factions. A guideline for dealing with differences can be useful. If two people or subgroups disagree, it may be more useful to have a guideline stating that they get together (sometimes with a mediator) outside of the meeting of the whole group to work out their differences rather than holding up the actions of the entire team. A third person or subunit could be appointed to listen to both sides of the issues and then recommend possible compromises or new alternatives. Time limits for the open discussion of differences might expedite reaching a conclusion (or might be a frustrating hindrance). A majority voting procedure might be appropriate if the group can honestly adopt a "loyal opposition" position that allows the people the right to disagree or vote differently but still implement actions. Whatever the method for discussion, understanding, and resolving issues, a guideline will provide a beginning for coping with the sensitive problem of differences that may occur.

*How Will We Ensure the Completion of Work?*    One of the major problems in working in groups (particularly of a committee or a task force) is the frustrating experience of some people coming unprepared or failing to complete assignments. How can the team face that issue constructively? The guidelines may state that no one will be given or will accept an assignment if the person honestly knows that he or she will not invest an appropriate amount of energy in its preparation. This means that there must be a realistic level of priority building and a climate of trust so that people will feel free to state their honest preferences and reactions to assignments. This guideline may outline a procedure for having the chairperson or other designated leader remind everyone with an assignment at a suitable time prior to the next meeting. An action summary of every meeting will clearly identify all assignments and dates for report and completion, as illustrated in the following sample.

### Action Summary (Sample)

| Decision | Who Is to Do What | Date for Completion | Date to Report Progress |
|---|---|---|---|
| 1. A training seminar for all supervisors will be held on June 15. | 1. John Hicks will make all physical arrangements. | June 10 | Next meeting— May 20 |
| | 2. Ann Stewart will contact the three possible resource people. | May 24 | Next meeting— May 20 |

The action summary can be used in place of or in addition to regular narrative minutes, but it should clearly pinpoint assignments and times for completion. The guideline may suggest an appropriate action, such as a personal visit by the chairperson, a report and explanation to the committee, or some other review mechanism, if a person fails to complete an assignment.

*How Will We Change Things that Are Not Producing Results?*   There should be some guidelines for reviewing the way the committee or team has been working and a method for making changes when guidelines or procedures or even people in certain positions are no longer achieving results. This guideline may suggest a periodic evaluation session at which the team honestly looks at its own work, reviews its successes and failures, and asks, What changes would make the team more effective? If guideline 3 had been operating effectively, many issues will have been covered, but the team may need to agree on a periodic review and evaluation meeting or that any person may call for such a meeting when he or she feels that conditions warrant it.

Again, the success of such a meeting depends on people feeling free to express their honest views about the team's effectiveness and to make recommendations for improvement. A fearful, defensive group will find it difficult to plan useful changes.

# 12

## Following Up

### What Happens After the Team-Building Session

An important aspect of the team-building process is follow-up. Too many team-building programs have failed, not because the initial sessions were ineffective but due to the lack of clear follow-up to ensure that the gains, agreements, and assignments made had been moved ahead.

### The Follow-Up Process

Assuming that a team-building program began with a block of time that resulted in some agreements to change or improve the way team members have been functioning, how does a good follow-up program proceed? There must be some method of following up with team members on assignments or agreements and then some form of continuing goal setting for improved performance. These follow-up activities can be done by the whole team together, one to one with team members, or a combination of the two. Fortunately some excellent research has been done that describes the kinds of follow-up processes that have proved to be successful.

Professor Wayne Boss[1] of the University of Colorado became interested in the "regression" effect following a team-building ses-

---

[1]R. Wayne Boss, "Team Building and the Problem of Regression: The Personal Management Interview as an Intervention," *Journal of Applied Behavioral Science 19*, no. 1 (1983) and a more extended discussion in the book by Boss, *Organization Development in Health Care* (Reading, Mass.: Addison-Wesley, 1989)

sion. He observed, as have others, that during a two- or three-day intensive team-building activity, people became very enthusiastic about making improvements but that within a few weeks, the spark had dwindled, and people had regressed to old performance levels. Boss wondered, "Is there a way to keep performance high following the team-building session and to prevent the regression phenomenon from occurring?" He began to experiment with a one-to-one follow-up meeting he called the Personal Management Interview (PMI). The PMI had two stages—first, a role negotiation meeting between boss and subordinate (usually one hour) during which both clarified their expectations of each other, what they needed from each other, and what they would eventually contract to do for each other.

Following the initial role negotiation session, the two parties met regularly. Boss found that these meetings had to be held on a regular basis (weekly, biweekly, or monthly), but if they were held and followed the agreed-on agenda, performance stayed up without regression for periods of up to three years. States Boss, "Without exception, the off-site level of group effectiveness was maintained only in those teams that employed the PMI, while the teams that did not use the PMI evidenced substantial regression in the months after their team-building sessions."

What goes on in these interviews that makes such a difference? Despite some variation, each interview tended to deal with the following issues:

- Discussion of any organizational or work problems facing the subordinate
- Training or coaching given by the supervisor to the subordinate
- Resolution of any concerns or problems between supervisor and subordinate
- Information sharing to bring the subordinate up to date on what is happening in the organization
- Discussion of any personal problems or concerns

These were common agenda items, but the first part of every meeting was spent in reviewing assignments and accomplishments since the last session. Time was also spent in making new assignments and agreeing on goals and plans to be reviewed at the next PMI. These assignments and agreements were written down, and both parties had a copy that was the basis of the review at the following meeting.

Boss has the following suggestions for conducting an effective PMI:

- The PMI is most effective when conducted in a climate of high support and trust. Establishing this climate is primarily the responsibility of the superior.

- The interview must be held on a regular basis and be free from interruptions.

- Both parties must prepare for the meeting by having an agreed-on agenda; otherwise, the PMI becomes nothing more than a "rap" session.

- When possible, a third party whom both the supervisor and the subordinate trust is present to take notes and record action items.

- Meetings are documented by use of a standard form on two-part carbonless paper. Both parties agree on the form.

- The leader must be willing to hold subordinates accountable and to ask the difficult "why" questions when assignments are not completed.

Boss has found that performance drops off if these meetings are not held but will increase if meetings are started, even if they had never been held before or had been stopped for a time. Certainly the evidence is compelling enough to indicate that this is an effective follow-up procedure.

The research by Boss does not talk about any further team sessions. Some units that have used the PMI have also reported having regular staff meetings to deal with issues common to all, as well as additional team-development sessions every three to six months. These later sessions identify any current problems or concerns and establish new change goals and plans for improvement.

In the past many teams have followed up a team-building session with additional team meetings to review progress. The advantage of the PMI is that it allows more time to talk with each person on an individual basis. If this were done in the presence of the whole team, it could be both inhibiting and extremely time consuming.

## Follow-Up Team Sessions

In his research on sales teams, Rensis Likert[2] has described the elements of follow-up team meetings that make a significant difference in the performance of team members—in this case, sales personnel. The research was done with sales offices from a national sales organization. The top twenty sales units were compared with the bottom twenty to see what made the difference. Likert found the following to be the most important factors:

- The team leader (the sales manager) had high personal performance goals and a plan for achieving those goals. Team members saw an example of high performance as they watched the team leader.

- The team leader displayed highly supportive behavior toward team members and encouraged them to support one another.

- The team leader used participative methods in supervision. That is, all team members were involved in helping the team and the members achieve their goals.

The major process for achieving high performance was holding regular, well-planned meetings of the sales team for review of each person's performance. In contrast to Boss's PMI, which is a one-to-one follow-up, the units in the Likert research used team meetings as the follow-up process. Those team meetings had the following major features:

- The team met regularly—every two weeks or every month.

- The size of the team varied but was usually between twelve and fifteen members.

- The sales manager presided over the meeting but allowed wide participation in the group. The main function of the manager was to keep the group focused on the task, push the group to set high performance goals, and discourage negative, nonsupportive, ego-deflating actions of team members.

---

[2]R. Likert, *The Human Organization* (New York: McGraw-Hill, 1967), Chapter 4.

- Each salesperson presented a report of his or her activities of the previous period, including a description of approach used, closings attempted, sales achieved, and volume and quality of total sales.
- All the other team members then analyzed the person's efforts and offered suggestions for improvement. Coaching was given by team members to one another.
- Each salesperson then announced his or her goals and procedures to be used for review at the next team meeting.

The researchers concluded that this form of team meeting resulted in four benefits:

- Salespeople set higher goals.
- They were more motivated to achieve their goals.
- They received more assistance, coaching, and help from boss and peers.
- The group got more new ideas on how to improve performance as people shared, not hid, their successful new methods.

Likert summarizes these team meetings this way:

These group meetings are effective when the manager (or supervisor) does a competent job of presiding over the interactions of the sales people. Appreciably poorer results are achieved whenever the manager himself analyzes each person's performance and results and sets goals for him. Such man-to-man interactions in the meetings, dominated by the manager, do not create group loyalty and have a far less favorable impact on the salesman's motivation than do group interactions and decision meetings. [p. 57]

It seems possible, then, to have either one-to-one follow-up meetings or a series of follow-up meetings as a way of maintaining high performance of team members. The key issue is that team building means a continuous effort to monitor the team's ability to implement actions designed to improve team performance. The key person is the team leader, who must build in some type of follow-up procedure.

Two follow-up methods are one-to-one interviews and follow-up team meetings. Other follow-up procedures are available, depending on the nature of the team's problems and plans.

It is possible to engage in a follow-up data-gathering process using some type of survey or questionnaire to see if the unit members feel the activities of the team have improved. Another approach is to have an outsider come in and interview members to check on what has improved and what actions are still needed. Alternatively, an outside observer could be invited to watch the team in action and give a process review at the end of the meeting.

If the problem of the team is poor interaction at meetings, it is possible to follow up with the use of a procedure to get reactions of people after each meeting or after some meetings. The team leaders could use either a type of quick, written form or ask for a critique of the meeting verbally, using the following questions: How satisfied were you with the team meeting today? Are there any actions we keep doing that restrict our effectiveness? What do we need to stop doing, start doing, or continue doing that would improve our team performance? Do we really function as a team, or are there indications that teamwork is lacking? Are we achieving our goals and using each person's resources effectively?

If these questions are discussed, sufficient time needs to be allotted to do an adequate critique. If a written form is used, it could be filled out and summarized, and the next team meeting could begin with a review of the summary and a discussion of what should be done in the current meeting to make the team more effective.

# 13

# Reducing Interteam Conflict

Thus far this book has focused on designs and methods for increasing the team effectiveness *within* a work unit. But often a major organizational problem is the lack of teamwork *between* units. In fact, units of organizations that become too cohesive and too self-involved and concerned may be ineffective in their working relationships with other units.

In their differentiation-integration model Lawrence and Lorsch have clearly demonstrated that units of organizations are and should be different.[1] When units have differing tasks, goals, personnel, time constraints, and structures, the functioning of these units is bound to be different. The issue is not how to make all units the same but how to develop an integrating process that allows these contrasting units to work together. One strategy for bringing greater integration between work units is an interteam development program.[2]

---

[1]P. R. Lawrence and J. W. Lorsch, *Organization and Environment: Managing Differentiation and Integration* (Boston: Division of Research, Harvard Business School, 1967).

[2]The basic theory and method for intergroup processes is found in R. Blake, H. Shepard, and J. Mouton, *Managing Intergroup Conflict in Industry* (Houston: Gulf, 1954). For other discussions on intergroup building strategies, see: J. K. Fordyce and R. Weil, *Managing with People* (Reading. Mass.: Addison-Wesley, 1971), pp. 123–130; R. Beckhard, *Organization Development: Strategies and Models* (Reading, Mass.: Addison-Wesley, 1969); E. H. Schein, *Organizational Psychology, Third Edition* (Englewood Cliffs, N.J.: Prentice-Hall, 1980), Chapter 5.

## Diagnosing the Problem

An interteam development program may be considered when two or more teams, which must collaborate for each to achieve its own unit's objective, experience one or more of the following conditions:

- Unit members avoid or withdraw from interactions with people from the other unit when they should be spending more working time together.
- The mutual product or end result desired by both units is delayed, diminished, blocked, or altered to the dissatisfaction of one or both parties.
- Needed services between units are not asked for.
- Services between units are not performed to the satisfaction of those units.
- Feelings of resentment or antagonism occur as a result of unit interactions.
- People feel frustrated, rejected, or misunderstood by those in the other unit with whom they must work.
- More time is spent in either avoiding or circumventing interaction with the other unit or internally complaining about the other unit than in working through mutual problems.

## Designing the Solution

If at least one of the managers in the dysfunctional unit interaction diagnoses the situation accurately and is willing to contact the other unit manager, an interunit team-development program may be proposed. It is necessary to get agreement of *both* units to move the program ahead. If the managers of the two groups agree to an interteam building process but do not get the commitment of their unit members, a great deal of resistance to the program is likely to result.

The goal of the program is to develop a problem-solving process that will reduce the existing dysfunctional interaction and allow future problems to be solved more effectively before a breakdown in unit interaction occurs. A number of design strategies can be used for planning and conducting the proposed program.

In preparation, members of both units should have the purpose and format of the program explained to them. This could be done by the manager involved or in conjunction with an outside facilitator. Agreements to participate should be achieved in both units.

Plans should be made for a block of time to get the appropriate people from both units to work on the interface problems. If the two units are small, it may be possible to involve all unit personnel. If units are larger, it may be necessary to have representatives work through the problem areas.

### Design A

1. Appropriate members from units X and Y meet to work out a more functional method of operating. Members are introduced, and the plan, purpose, and schedule of the program are reviewed.

2. Ground rules are established. The essential ground rule is for people to adopt a problem-solving stance. The issue is to work out a solution, not to accuse or fix blame. Participants should agree to look at the behavior of their own group members and identify times when their own members are trying to accuse, fix blame, or defend a position rather than solve the problem.

3. Unit members *in their own groups* begin work on the following task. On sheets of newsprint, answer the following:

   a) What actions does the other unit engage in that create problems for us? List them.

   b) What actions do we engage in that we think may create problems for them? List them.

   c) What recommendations would we make to improve the situation?

4. Each unit brings its sheets of paper and gives them to the other unit to review.

5. Time is allotted for each unit to review the work of the other unit and to ask questions for clarification. Agreements and disparities in the two lists are noted.

6. Members of the two units are now put into *mixed teams* composed of an equal number of members from both

units. The first task is for each team to review the lists and come up with an agreed-on list of the major problems or obstacles that keep the two units from functioning together effectively. Each mixed team presents its list of problems to the total group, and the results are tabulated. The major agreed-on problems are then identified and listed.

7. Members return to the mixed teams. Each mixed team is given one of the problems identified to work out a recommended solution. This should include what the problem is, what actions should be taken, who should be responsible for what actions, what the time schedule is, and how to keep the problem from occurring again.

8. Mixed teams bring their solutions back to the total group for review and agreement, particularly from those who must implement the actions.

### Design B

This design is similar to A but is a "fishbowl" design. Instead of the two teams doing their work alone and then presenting the sheets to each other, each unit discusses its issue *in front of* the other group.

1. Group X sits together in a circle. Group Y sits outside and observes and listens. Group X members discuss the three questions listed in item 3 of design A. A recorder writes down the points of discussion.

2. Group Y now moves into the center circle. Group X observes and listens.

3. Following the fishbowl discussions, mixed teams are formed and perform the same tasks as in design A.

### Design C

A variation on designs A and B is to have the units discuss different questions. The designs are the same; only the questions are different.

1. How do we see the other unit? What is our image of them?

2. How do we think the other unit sees us? What is their image of us?

3. Why do we see them the way we do?
4. Why do we think they see us as we think they do?
5. What would have to change so we would have a more positive image and interaction with each other?

### Design D

1. An outside facilitator interviews members of both units privately prior to the team-development session. He or she tries to identify the problems between the units, the source of the problems, and people's recommended solutions.
2. The facilitator summarizes the results of these interviews at the interteam meeting. The summaries are printed or posted for all to see.
3. Mixed teams from both units review the summary findings and list the major areas they feel need to be resolved. Major ideas are agreed on by the total group.
4. Mixed teams devise recommended solutions to the problem assigned to them.

### Design E

This design involves selecting a mixed task force composed of members from both units. The job of the task force is to review the interface problems and then recommend solutions to the problems for both groups to consider and agree on.

1. Representatives of the task force are selected in the following manner: Team X lists *all* of its group members who the group feels could adequately represent them on the task force and gives this list to team Y. Team Y then selects the three or four members from team X. Both units engage in this listing and selecting process. The result is a mixed task force composed of members agreeable to both units.
2. The task force may wish to either interview people from the other units or invite a facilitator to work with it. Whatever the working style, the task force is asked to come up with the major conditions blocking interteam effectiveness, what actions should be taken, who should be responsible for what actions, a time frame, how these problems can be prevented from oc-

curring again, or what method will be used for solving other problems that may arise.

### Design F

A forcefield model could be used by any combination of the two teams. They agree that the current level of functioning is not adequate. Then they agree they need to improve to a higher level of cooperation. The two groups list and agree on the major restraining and driving forces. In subgroups they look at the major forces and develop actions for dealing with these forces agreeable to all.

### Follow-Up

What happens if the two units have new or recurring problems in the future? There needs to be some method for dealing with new concerns as they arise.

It is possible to go through one of the six designs again. It is also possible to establish a review board made up of members of both groups. The function of this group is to examine the problem and come 'up with a recommended solution or procedure that would then be accepted by both units.

---

## Choosing an Appropriate Model

Given the variety of interteam building models available, what determines which model would be most appropriate? One factor to consider is the confidence and competence of the unit managers to conduct such a program alone, without the help of an outside facilitator. If they choose to conduct the session alone, it would be wise to select an alternative that is simple, easy to communicate to others, and has minimal chance for slippage in implementation. Design E—the selection of an interteam task force—is the most traditional way to work on the interteam problems and is probably the easiest alternative to implement without help. It is also the design that has the least involvement of all the members of the two groups and may have the least impact, at least initially.

Design A probably is the most straightfcrward problem-solving format, with the least possibility of surfacing conflicts and issues that could erupt into an unproductive rehash of old grievances. The fishbowl design may create reactions to individuals as they are observed that may be difficult to handle without a trained facilitator. Similarly, approaching the issue through an examination of mutual images (design C) may also give rise to feelings and reactions that may be disruptive to one not used to handling such concerns.

## Conclusions

Intergroup problems open up the issues about the unit to which one has commitment and definition of the ultimate "team." In modern organizations it is not enough to build intense loyalty into the work unit or department, particularly at the expense of the larger organization. Unless people in different departments that must collaborate can see the larger picture and understand that the team is more than the small group, intergroup conflicts can and do emerge. Team-building sessions *between* units can be conducted before problems occur to cement relationships and establish working guidelines. Certainly it is important to get work units together and iron out difficulties when intergroup problems occur. Single-unit loyalty can be detrimental to achieving the organization's goal.

# 14

# Where Does Team Building Go from Here?

The use of teams in organizations has almost exploded in the past few years. Managers are setting up teams for all kinds of uses, but the success rate has been less than spectacular. Many specialists working in the field of team building believe that until the use of teams, collaboration, and teamwork become a part of the basic culture of the organization, the impact of going through team-building efforts will be minimal.

Organizations that want to gain the advantages that result from the synergy of teamwork must first go through a major reexamination of the basic assumptions of the organization to see if the ideal values that are articulated are congruent with the way the culture is presented in the behavior of administrators and managers at all levels. Then an examination of the internal systems must begin to see if the major parts of the administrative system (review, rewards, career development) and the sociotechnical system are supportive of the culture. If these two key aspects are congruent, work must be done to ensure that people are hired and trained so they can function effectively in this new organizational environment.

This major organizational overhaul is very difficult to achieve. Time, resources, and the strong commitment of top management are required. Unfortunately current accounting and financial practices are geared to the short term, and stakeholders often want to see immediate profit/loss results and therefore push organization leaders to make short-term, profit-oriented decisions. The current trend in organizations is to meet crisis situations by downsizing rather than by engaging in major organizational review and change. Then to meet the negative impacts of downsizing, there is a call for people to come together and become part of the "whole team" or to try and get people to become part of the smaller work teams. When this is done and employees see that the basic culture and systems have not changed, they will react with increased cynicism and increased passive resistance to efforts trying to get people to get excited about "teamwork."

My own experience in working with large international organizations is that this type of major change rarely takes place, and the probability is high that the use of various kinds of teams will continue for a time until a new idea or program or concept becomes the next panacea for organizational ills. The resistance to organizational change is compounded by both the short-term accounting procedures and the traditional method of leadership succession. People in top-management positions tend to advance and reward those whose management philosophy and style are similar to their own. People who aspire to move up the management career ladder become very adept at conforming to the norms that seem to prescribe how a person gets ahead in the management game. It takes tremendous courage for a CEO to shift out of the traditional pattern, ignore short-term pressures, and engage in the tough process of real organizational change.

***Business Schools.***   I wrote the following in the second edition and believe that the situation has not changed much:

> Business schools that should be teaching young men and women how to work in teams give lip service to the process but do not know how to teach these skills to prospective organizational managers and workers. The professors may put students into study or project teams and grade the team product but will spend no time at all in helping these students understand how a good team functions and how to manage the group problems that may arise. [Note: I believe that one reason for this lack is that very few professors know anything about group processes and how to teach them.] The end result is that usually a few students take over and get the group paper or project completed while others goof off or slide along and get rewarded for the efforts of others. This leaves many students with a

negative feeling about team activities as they leave school and go into the work force.

Much of the educative process represents the same condition that exists in the world of work: Students are put into teams of various kinds but are rewarded for individual effort, and at times their efforts to collaborate are called "cheating." The teachers do not know how to teach team processes but use teams without understanding what they are doing in this area. When students then move from school to work, they find exactly the same practices they have experienced before.

*Training.* In the past organizations have expected their human resources departments, particularly those involved in training and development, to set up training programs to teach mangers how to build teams. With the current emphasis on teamwork, this practice will continue with a minimum of success, since all of the training people know they are training people in actions that are contrary to the culture and will not be rewarded in the systems.

Often the HR people have this insight but are in positions of low power and influence, and their counsel is not asked for by those in the strategic power positions. HR people must be able to have a training process that will in fact teach mangers and team members how to function effectively in teams. Additionally, however, they need to be able to show power people to what extent the training is antithetical to the culture and the systems. This means doing some basic research examining culture, systems, and training and then being able to present hard data to decision makers.

My personal view is that teamwork is essential to the effective functioning of people in organizations. Research has long shown that productivity and morale are impacted by effective or ineffective teamwork. I hope that my pessimism for the future of team building is unfounded. It is my own guess that there will still be spectacular cases of success when a crisis and a strong leader result in making some major changes in the way the organization is structured and functions. Others will read about these successes and will want to apply the "quick fix" and will set up teams because this is the smart thing or the "in" thing to do. To begin to build a truly collaborative society, teamwork in its best sense must be practiced in the home, the schools, the churches, and the workplace. People must experience what it is like to be part of a truly effective team in many parts of their lives. Those who work in groups must reexamine the ways they are functioning together and engage in new ways to solve problems and get goals accomplished. The use of real teams is the only way I know to ensure that people feel that they have influence over the key aspects of their lives, can shape their world, and can find growth and satisfaction.